Cathe₁

Last Empress of Russia

By Michael W. Simmons

Table of Contents

Chapter One: Princess Sophie

"Fortune is not as blind as people imagine. It is often the result of a series of precise and well-chosen steps that precede events and are not perceived by the common herd. In people it is also more specifically the result of qualities, of character, and of personal conduct. To make this more concrete, I will make the following syllogism of it: Qualities and character will be the major premise. Conduct, the minor. Fortune or misfortune, the conclusion."

preface to the memoirs of Catherine II of Russia

Birth and childhood

On November 8, 1727, at the age of 38, Prince Christian August of Anhalt-Zerbst was married to Princess Johanna Elizabeth of Holstein-Gottorp, who was 15. Despite his rank and title, Christian August was not exceptionally wealthy, nor was he fashionable or powerful; he was just one of many minor princes who ruled the many minor principalities and territories that would, some hundred years in the future, become united under the Prussian king Wilhelm I to form the German empire. Christian August served the present king of Prussia, Frederick the Great, as a military officer, and his military career was the most distinguished thing about him, apart from his strict Lutheran religious principles. He was not well-acquainted with Johanna before her marriage. Like most wealthy minor noblemen, he married simply to produce an heir. He was fortunate to claim a daughter of the Holstein-Gottorp family, whose far-flung relations and family connections included the Russian royal family, but he was not fated to be happy with his new wife.

Johanna Elizabeth found herself disappointed in the match that had been arranged for her, and by the unambitious mode of living that Christian August insisted upon. Shortly after their marriage, they moved to Stettin, where Christian August had been awarded the command of a regiment. It was a boring little town on the Bay of Pomerania, in what is now Poland, and the social life of its upper-class inhabitants revolved around dull military-oriented functions. Johanna had been raised by her godmother, the Duchess of Brunswick, at her court in northern Germany, where clothes were always in fashion, and gossip was always fresh; Christian August's modest and strict way of life was boring, repressive, and incomprehensible to his teenaged wife.

Princess Johanna gave birth to the couple's first child on May 2, 1729, about a year and a half after her marriage, when she was only sixteen. She was expecting a son, and the appearance of her daughter came as a profound disappointment. Johanna named the baby girl Sophia Fredericka August, and immediately lost all interest in her. The infant was given over to the care of a French Huguenot woman named Elisabeth Cardel, who had fled to Germany in search of more tolerant religious climes, and gained employment in the Anhalt-Zerbst family as a governess. Cardel, known as "Babette" to her charge, was to supervise the young princess's education until her marriage. She is credited with instilling the intellectual habits for which the Empress Catherine would become famous.

Despite her disappointment at not having given birth to a son, Johanna was determined that her daughter would serve her ambitions to the extent possible, namely by making the illustrious marriage that she herself had failed to make. Despite Christian August's modest standards of living, Princess Johanna gave the young Sophie the education and social graces that would prepare her for life at any of the royal courts in Europe. Sophie was a clever child, and she took eagerly to the lessons taught by Babette and her tutor. She received instruction in etiquette and protocol, music, dancing, horseback riding, geography, history, and religion. She was clever enough to baffle and frustrate the Lutheran pastor her father employed to teach her these latter three subjects, particularly when it came to religion. She could not understand how God could allow for people to be condemned to hell who had lived and died prior to the birth of Christ, or how a supposedly loving and benevolent God could destroy the world in fire as it was prophesied in the Bible. Her tutor, unequipped to deal with such probing, precocious questions, threatened to beat her as punishment, and would have done so without the intervention of Babette.

While her governess was understanding of the child Sophie's intellectual curiosity, her mother was not. Princess Sophie's future career depended on her mother's ability to mold her flawlessly into the ideal princess-in-waiting, and too much independence of spirit could only interfere with that goal. Furthermore, Princess Johanna had never been fond of her, and the gulf between mother and daughter only widened when Sophie's brother, Wilhelm Christian, who was younger than her by about a year, died at the age of twelve. Johanna vented her feelings of loss, frustration, and annoyance by repeatedly telling Sophie that she was ugly and unattractive, and by forcing her to keep silent and debase herself in displays of humility whenever visitors arrived. Perhaps Sophie's most remarkable trait was her ability to control her anger and pride and comply with her mother's domineering demands. These lessons would stand Sophie in excellent stead when she traveled to the Russian court of Empress Elizabeth I, another domineering woman who, for years, would control her life completely.

The young princess

Princess Johanna, having married slightly beneath her, might easily have lost touch with her powerful and royally-connected friends from childhood; but she knew that her marital aspirations for her daughter depended on cultivating those attachments, so she returned yearly to the court of Brunswick, taking Sophie with her once she was old enough for the journey. Marriages amongst the aristocracy were often arranged while one or both parties were still small children, so it suited the elder princess's purposes to display her little daughter, with her all her education and accomplishments, to her friends who might have sons of their own to marry off. Sophie had been told so often that there was nothing attractive about her appearance that she forced herself to work all the harder at attracting people with her personal virtues, like modesty, patience, kindness, intelligence, and learning. She was a willing partner in her mother's efforts to find her an illustrious husband. She had witnessed firsthand the fates of women of her social rank who did not marry, in the persons of her mother's sisters, old maids who were cloistered together or shut away in the draftiest and oldest parts of their family's ancient castles. She had no desire to end up in the same condition.

It was on one of these visits to Johanna's relations that the young Princess Sophie first met her uncle's ward, Charles Peter Ulrich, the Duke of Holstein. Charles Peter was 11, only a year older than Sophie; he also happened to be the heir to the Swedish throne, as well as the only living grandson of Peter I of Russia, known to history as Peter the Great. Upon the death of Charles Peter's parents, he had been sent to live with Johanna's brother; by blood, he was Sophie's second cousin. He was not an especially prepossessing boy. As a pre-teen, he was already given to drunkenness and over-indulging at mealtimes, and unlike his intellectual cousin, he cared little for reading or the lessons of his tutors. But he accepted Sophie as a playmate, and this mark of favor was readily noticed by Johanna.

Later in life, as the Empress Catherine II, she recorded her recollections of young Charles Peter in her memoirs:

"I saw Peter III for the first time when he was eleven years old, in Eutin at the home of his guardian, the Prince Bishop of Lübeck... I was ten years old at the time. It was then that I heard it said among this assembled family that the young duke was inclined to drink, that his attendants found it difficult to prevent him from getting drunk at meals, that he was restive and hotheaded and did not like his attendants and especially Brümmer, and that otherwise he showed vivacity, but had a delicate and sickly appearance. In truth, his face was pale in color and he seemed to be thin and of a delicate constitution. His attendants wanted to give this child the appearance of a mature man, and to this end they hampered and restrained him, which could only inculcate falseness in his conduct as well as his character."

It would seem that Princess Sophie had no very flattering impression of the man to whom she would one day be married, but by the time she was writing her memoirs Peter III was dead, and her memories of this first meeting were no doubt influenced by the uncomfortable years of marriage they had passed through together.

Princess Sophie was well-liked in the royal courts of northern Germany where her mother passed most of her time. Few other people shared Johanna's low opinion of her daughter's appearance or her charms; indeed, she was far more popular with her mother's friends than Johanna was herself. Sophie demonstrated extraordinary political instincts from a very young age. She knew how to make herself liked. People were attracted to her because she listened attentively and said little; Sophie enjoyed the advantage of having cultivated their favor while learning little details about them that they had perhaps not meant to reveal.

By the time Sophie was a teenager, she was considered pretty, bright, gracious, and amiable by everyone who knew her, but she concealed a secret ambition: eager though she was for a good marriage, her principle goal was to escape the control of her domineering, borderline abusive mother. This, perhaps, is the reason she briefly considered the suit of the first man to ask for her hand in marriage: her own uncle, Johanna's younger brother. Ten years older than Sophie, he proposed to her, abruptly and in private, when she was fourteen. When she expressed confusion, he declared that their blood relationship was no obstacle to their union; amongst aristocratic families, such marriages were not unheard of. Sophie had never before considered him a potential match, but she accepted his proposal on the grounds that her parents gave their permission— permission that she must have known would not be forthcoming, not when Johanna still cherished hopes of marrying Sophie off to a royal heir. It is possible, however, that she might have been willing to go through with the marriage if permission had been given; many a young girl has accepted the first eligible proposal they received out of nothing more than the desire to be independent of her parents.

An arranged marriage

Just as Sophie's uncle was proposing marriage to his teenage niece, Sophie's mother received a message from the Imperial court of Russia that was to change her family's destiny forever. The most valuable of all Princess Johanna's high family connections was her relationship with Empress Elisabeth of Russia, daughter of Peter the Great, who had seized the throne in a coup d'etat in 1742. As a young woman, Elisabeth had been engaged to be married to Johanna's elder brother; she was extremely fond of him, and when he died of smallpox a few weeks before the wedding, she was heartbroken. Furthermore, Elisabeth's older sister Anne had been briefly married to Johanna's brother; the young Charles Peter Ulrich was the only child of their union. Johanna had taken pains to cultivate this family connection by gifting the empress with a portrait of the deceased Anne, and by asking Elisabeth to become godmother to her youngest daughter, Sophie's sister.

In 1743, about a year after Elisabeth came to the throne, she had her nephew, the young Charles Peter, brought to St. Petersburg to be invested as her heir. This meant that he could no longer inherit the Swedish throne, but according to the terms of the Treaty of Åbo, which settled the dynastic connections between Sweden and Russia, Elisabeth was permitted to appoint another heir to take his place. The person she designated as the future king of Sweden was Adolphus Frederick of the Holstein family, who had been Charles Peter's guardian. He was also the brother of Elisabeth's dead fiancé—and thus, the brother of Johanna.

Elisabeth's distinguishing Johanna's family in this manner renewed all of the mother's hopes for her daughter making an important marriage. The family was elevated even further when Sophie's father, Christian August, inherited the principality of Anhalt-Zerbst jointly with his brother. Anhalt-Zerbst was extremely small, but it was independent, and

Johanna thus found herself the wife of the ruler of a sovereign state, entitled to be addressed as "Her Highness". Shortly after Johanna's family moved to their small ancestral palace, she received a letter from Otto Brümmer, a marshal of the Russian Imperial court, informing her that the Empress wished for her to come to St. Petersburg—and to bring her daughter Sophie along with her. There could only be one possible reason for such a summons, and though the letter did not specify that Elisabeth was considering a match between Sophie and Charles Peter (now Grand Duke Peter), another letter arriving swiftly on the heels of the first did. This second letter was from Frederick II, King of Prussia. It read:

"I will no longer conceal the fact that in addition to the respect I have always cherished for you and for the princess your daughter, I have always had the wish to bestow some unusual good fortune upon the latter, and the thought came to me that it might be possible to arrange a match for her with her cousin, the Grand Duke Peter of Russia."

There was one condition attached to this very exciting invitation: Sophie's father, Christian August, was explicitly excluded from the visit. Furthermore, by writing to Johanna and not to her husband, Frederick of Prussia was guilty of a serious insult. There was no reason or explanation given for both Frederick and Elisabeth slighting the Prince of Anhalt-Zerbst in this way, but the motive must have been obvious: Christian August was famous for his strict Lutheran principles, and it was reasonable to assume that he would have had serious objections to his daughter making a marriage that would require her to change her religion. The religion of the Imperial court was that of the Russian Orthodox Church, and if Sophie was indeed to marry the grand duke, she would have to convert.

Christian August had another objection to the marriage: Russia was a dangerous and politically unstable country with a harsh climate. Europeans viewed it as barely a step above a savage wasteland. Only a hundred years before, the fashions, music, literature, and styles of the European royal courts were unknown in the vast, distant kingdom of the tsars. Russian nobles still adorned themselves in long "Eastern-style" robes and full waist-length beards. Women were kept cloistered all their lives, even after their marriage, and did not participate in society. Peter the Great had ushered in modernizing reforms over the strenuous protests of his nobles, requiring that they adopt a European mode of dress and shave their beards. This was no light undertaking during the Russian winters; the long traditional robes offered an insulation against the cold that the more fashionable doublet and hose did not. But the Emperor was determined to drag his court out of the medieval era and into the 16th century; if his nobles did not cut their beards, Peter would grab them by the chin and cut it off for them with his knife. Peter I's reign had seen several revolts and rebellions, and his daughter, the present empress, had seized the

Russian throne from Peter's niece, Anna of Courland, who was regent for the boy emperor Ivan VI, now a prisoner. Elizabeth wished to see the grand duke married to a European princess like Sophie in part because it meant she would not have to choose an Imperial bride from amongst the various powerful Russian families that formed the factions of her court. Should this attempt to maintain the balance of power backfire, however, another rebellion might break out, and Elizabeth and her heirs be deposed. Sophie herself was not likely to survive such a purge. Christian August was therefore painfully aware that by sending his daughter to Russia he might be sending her to her death.

Johanna, however, cared for none of these concerns. She was beside herself with delight. When Elisabeth's letter reached her, she immediately sent word to Russia that she and Sophie were on their way, and that only the lack of wings prevented them from flying there. The journey north was extremely dangerous at that time of year, but Johanna counted the danger as nothing compared to the prospect of enjoying her royal patron's favor in person. Elisabeth had sent 10,000 rubles to Johanna to fund her journey to Russia, and Johanna, who seemed to regard her daughter as a mere afterthought in the proceedings, spent almost the whole sum on lavish new dresses for herself. Sophie's wardrobe consisted of three dresses, a few handkerchiefs, and some old linen—a miserably poor showing for a prospective Imperial bride. It was, unfortunately, characteristic of the elder princess's narcissism that she did not consider how it would look for her to be so well-dressed when her daughter was standing next to her, humbly attired.

This was not the end of Johanna's lack of consideration for Sophie's feelings. For almost a week after the arrival of the empress's letter, a week filled with frantic preparations for the long, perilous journey, neither she nor her husband bothered to inform Sophie that she was going to Russia to be married. Sophie, however, figured it out for herself. She was clever and observant, and she knew why her mother had so assiduously cultivated her ties with the Russian court. And she remembered the Grand Duke Peter from when they were children together; she had always been aware that he was a potential match for her. By Elisabeth's orders, the journey had to be undertaken in the utmost secrecy. They could not even tell anyone where they were going, much less why. It is possible that Sophie's parents, underestimating the resolute character of their daughter, feared that she would not be able to keep the secret if she knew what was to happen. But it was Johanna who could not keep secrets from Sophie, who had glimpsed the letter after its arrival. She had spotted suggestive keywords, such as "Russia" and "your eldest daughter" before it was taken away to her father's study, and it wasn't long before she put the pieces together on her own.

Any other girl of 14, especially one who had so recently been contemplating marriage with another

16

man, might have balked at the prospect of being sent so far away from her home and everything she knew to be married off to a near-stranger in a country with foreign language, customs, and religion. But when Sophie confronted her mother with her suspicions, and was finally informed of the fate that had been decided for her, she professed herself unafraid. Neither the dangerous journey, nor the prospect of living in Russia for the remainder of her life, dismayed her. When parents are restrictive and controlling, teenage children are frequently rebellious, but at this point in Sophie's life her goal was the same as her mother's. Not only would this marriage make her an empress consort, but once she married, she would no longer be under her mother's control. Even if Johanna failed to think this far ahead, it is certain that Sophie did not.

Audience with Frederick II

The first stop which the two Holstein princesses made on their journey to Russia was at the court of Frederick II, King of Prussia, at his express invitation. Unbeknownst to Sophie or her mother, Frederick stood to gain or lose a great deal as a result of her marriage to the Grand Duke Peter. Shortly after he had succeeded to the Prussian throne, Frederick had gone to war against Maria Theresa of Austria. In the 18th century, the German states were scattered and geographically divided, lacking contiguous borders; in other words, Prussia controlled territories that lay on either side of territories controlled by other kingdoms. To consolidate Prussia's military dominance, Frederick sent troops to Silesia in 1742, occupying it without resistance. Much to his surprise, the young and beautiful Austrian empress raised arms against him, locking him into a conflict that would last for much of his reign. Frederick was anxious to avoid a scenario in which Austria allied with Russia against him—a very real danger, because Elisabeth's vice-chancellor, Count Alexis Bestuzhev-Ryumin, was deeply antipathetic towards Prussia, and wished to make an alliance between Russia, England, Holland, and Austria. Frederick felt that his best chance of winning Elisabeth's loyalty against the Austrians lay in her nephew's marrying a German princess. He was therefore eager to meet Princess Sophie and get an idea of her character; though she could not be expected to play an influential role in politics until she was much older, he hoped that she would be an ally to him one day.

When Johanna and Sophie arrived in Berlin in 1744, Johanna lost no time in presenting herself at Frederick's court—alone, without her daughter. Again, she seemed to lose all sight of the fact that it was Sophie, not herself, who by rights ought to take center-stage in unfolding events. Johanna attempted to excuse herself for not bringing Sophie to court by saying that she had no dresses suitable for appearing in the royal presence—conveniently omitting to mention that Sophie lacked such formal attire because Johanna herself had spent all of their money on her own wardrobe. Frederick, impatient with her behavior, asked his sister to lend Sophie a gown, and invited the young princess to dine with him. Just as Sophie's father had been omitted from the marital negotiations, Frederick omitted Johanna from the dinner invitation; one can only guess how Johanna reacted in private to such a slight.

Princess Sophie made her first and only appearance at the court of Frederick the Great in a borrowed, ill-fitting dress, devoid of flowers or jewelry or any of the other adornments that were fashionable for ladies of the court—in short, with nothing but her wits and intelligence to recommend her. Though shy at first, unused to being singled out or preferred above her mother, she made a highly favorable impression on the Prussian king. Frederick was a great lover of music and an accomplished flautist; Sophie was able to make intelligent conversation with him about music and opera and literature. Later in life, she wrote that Frederick had drawn her out on a number of subjects that adults did not normally expect children to understand. She was, for the first time in her life, being treated seriously as a future player in the royal politics of Europe, rather than as a mere adjunct to her dominating mother. Frederick sent his favorable impressions of Sophie to the Empress Elisabeth, writing that, "The little princess of Zerbst combines the gaiety and spontaneity natural to her age with intelligence and wit surprising in one so young."

Fredrick had another purpose for bringing Johanna and Sophie to Berlin. After satisfying himself that Sophie was well-qualified to be a future empress-consort, he drew her mother aside for a private conversation. He imparted to Johanna that Count Bestuzhev, being prejudiced against a Russo-Prussian alliance, would be actively working against her from the moment she arrived at court, and that he would attempt to prevent the marriage from taking place by any means possible. Could he, Frederick, trust Johanna to represent the interests of Prussia abroad, not only by bringing her daughter's marriage about, but by winning Elisabeth's favor towards himself? Johanna, perpetually desperate to feel distinguished and important, did not stop to consider the dangerous position she would place herself and Sophie in by getting involved in Russian court politics in this way. She was all too delighted to feel that she had a primary purpose in making the journey to Russia, as a secret representative of the Prussian king, and not merely as her daughter's guardian. She promised to do her utmost, despite the fact that her husband, Christian August, had made a special point of warning her not to become embroiled in politics.

When their visit to the court of Frederick the Great was concluded, Christian August accompanied his wife and daughter a little further on their journey, leaving them at last on the banks of the Oder River. Christian loved his daughter as Johanna never had, and both he and Sophie seemed to realize that there was little chance of their ever meeting again, because their parting was difficult and emotional. Sophie attempted to ease the sting of their parting by writing her father a letter in which she promised to cling to her Lutheran faith if at all possible:

"My Lord: I beg you to assure yourself that your advice and exhortation will remain forever engraved on my heart, as the seeds of the holy faith will in my soul, to which I pray God to lend all the strength it will need to sustain me through the temptations to which I expect to be exposed...I hope to have the consolation of being worthy of it, and likewise of continuing to receive good news of my dear Papa, and I am as long as I live, and in an inviolable respect, my lord, your Highness's most humble, most obedient, and faithful daughter and servant. Sophia."

It is probable that Sophie was merely seeking to offer her devout Lutheran father some consolation; when it came to religious matters she was more pragmatic than faithful, as her childhood battles with her religion tutor demonstrate. When the time came, Sophie would devote herself to the study of the Orthodox rite and the seeming sincerity of her conversion would win her a great deal of favor in the Russian court.

Elisabeth, Empress of Russia

On February 4, 1744, Johanna, traveling under the assumed name of the Countess of Reinbeck, and Sophie crossed the border from Lithuania into Russia. They had suffered a long, frozen, grueling journey by carriage over rocky, neglected postal roads that were normally traversed only by snow-sledge; despite the freezing temperatures, no snow had fallen, making the trip immensely more difficult. Frederick had sent a retinue to accompany them, but the journey took them to such remote locations that not even the king's name could command much in the way of comfort or privilege. They often had to sleep on the floor of remote huts, bundled under furs. The journey grew easier once they reached the Russian border, where Elisabeth's representative met them with a fur-lined coach to convey them the rest of the way to the Imperial court in St. Petersburg. There, at the Winter Palace, Johanna and Sophie were gifted with wardrobes that were suitable for the fierce Russian winters, and shortly afterwards they proceeded to Moscow, where Elisabeth was waiting, to celebrate the grand duke's sixteenth birthday.

The circumstances by which Peter came to be named heir to the Russian throne were convoluted, tied as they were to the upheavals which had made Elisabeth empress. Elisabeth was one of twelve children born to Peter the Great and his peasant wife, the woman who succeeded him after his death as Catherine I. Of this brood, only Elisabeth and her older sister Anne had survived to see the age of seven. Peter the Great had been given little in the way of formal education, but he took great care with the education of his daughters, to whom he was a devoted father. Both Elisabeth and Anne were considered great beauties and intelligent pupils; Anne learned to speak at least four languages, and Elisabeth was trained in the history, language, and courtly manners of France, reflecting Peter's hope of arranging a marriage between her and the French king Louis XV, who was within a few months of Elisabeth in age and had inherited his throne at the age of five. Despite Elisabeth's beauty and enormous popularity in her homeland, however, the French were unimpressed by the fact that her mother had been a peasant who was married to her father in secret on an uncertain date; they regarded Elisabeth as a possible bastard, unsuitable for the French throne.

One of Peter the Great's most remarkable legacies—the one which would ultimately make possible Catherine's remarkable career as his successor—was that he declared women to be eligible for the line of the Imperial succession. As Robert Massie writes,

"In a decree in February 1722, Peter had denounced as a dangerous practice, unfounded in scripture, the rule of male primogeniture, the ancient, time-honored sequence by which the grand dukes of Muscovy and later the Russian tsars had passed down the throne from father to eldest son. Henceforth, Peter declared, every reigning sovereign would have the power to designate his or her successor. Following his proclamation, Peter placed a crown on [his wife, Catherine I's] head and declared her empress."

The results of this decree had a profound impact on the next seventy-four years of Russian history. Until Catherine the Great was succeeded by her son, Paul I, who brought an end to female sovereignty and succession through the female line, the Russian throne was occupied chiefly by women. Peter the Great's peasant wife, Marta Helene Skowrońska, succeeded him as Catherine I; she reigned for less than two years before she too died, and the throne passed to the 11-year-old Peter II, grandson of Peter the Great by his first wife. Elisabeth befriended and supported her young half-brother, and though she was his designated successor according to the will of Catherine I, she made no attempt to infringe upon his authority.

When Peter II died of smallpox at the age of fourteen, there appeared a window of opportunity during which the then twenty-year-old Elisabeth might have made a successful bid for the throne. She was, after all, the legal heir. But Elisabeth felt that she was still too young and unready for such responsibility, and she declined to press her advantage. Both her mother and her fiancé, Johanna of Holstein's brother, had died only a few years before, and her beloved older sister Anne had recently been married and sent to Germany. Thus bereft of all the most important people in her life, Elisabeth was content to live in relative obscurity and pledge her loyalty to the new empress, Anna I, who was the daughter of Peter the Great's feeble-minded brother and co-tsar, Ivan.

Anna was fearful of Elisabeth from the first moments of her reign. Not only was Elisabeth's claim on the throne at least as strong as hers, but Elisabeth was more beloved by the people. This was only partly because she was the daughter of the revered Peter the Great. Apolitical though she was in her younger years, Elisabeth had high spirits and a genuine love of people, and she made herself enormously popular by mingling with the soldiers in the guard houses, and by flirting and taking lovers as she pleased. (Under her half sister's reign, there was no longer any possibility that a royal marriage would be arranged for her, and Elisabeth took advantage of the freedom this afforded her in her personal relationships. In Russia, this was not the great scandal it would have been in any of the royal courts of Europe.) In general, Elisabeth brought to the minds of all who knew her the best qualities of her heroic father. The Empress Anna feared her for good reason. Though Russian by birth, she surrounded herself with German advisors, and the Russian people were suspicious of this foreign element at court. Elisabeth, by contrast, was purely and wholeheartedly Russian.

The Empress Anna named as her successor the son of her niece, a German princess, Anna of Courland, whom she had brought to court, and who had converted to the Orthodox church before marrying a German prince. When Empress Anna died in October of 1740, the infant Ivan, only three months old, was named tsar, with his mother, Anna of Courland, acting as regent. This Anna was even more threatened by Elisabeth than the old empress had been; as regent, she carried the same foreign taint of German blood, and was even less popular with the commoners. Though Elisabeth tried to keep on friendly terms with Anna during her regency, Anna placed increasing restrictions on Elisabeth's finances and movements; there were even rumors that she intended to imprison Elisabeth in a convent and force her to become a nun.

On November 24, 1741, Elisabeth's closest advisor, a French doctor by the name of Armand Lestocq, came to see her with a piece of paper. On one side, he had drawn a picture of Elisabeth, a crowned empress; on the reverse, he had drawn a picture of her in a nun's veils, surrounded by instruments of torture. He told her that the moment had come for her to choose between these two destinies. That night, Elisabeth went to the barracks of the Preobrazhensky Regiment, a guard regiment of the Russian Imperial Army created by her father, Peter the Great. Since her father's death, she had visited their barracks frequently, dispensing favors, listening to their stories, drinking with them, and acting as godmother to their children. For this, and for her father's sake, they were willing to pledge Elisabeth their unswerving loyalty. She had only to enter their guardhouse and inform them that the moment had come; they immediately arrayed themselves at her back and marched for the Winter Palace. Elisabeth herself woke the sleeping regent to inform her that she had been deposed after a tenure of only thirteen months. When Anna begged for mercy for herself and her son, Elisabeth assured her that they would be spared. She kept her word; though the family was held prisoner until the end of Elisabeth's life, and Ivan was held separately from his parents and siblings after he turned twelve, they were not executed. Ivan would live until 1764, when insurrectionists during the reign of Catherine II attempted to free him and restore him to the throne; he was murdered before the plot could become successful on secret orders from Catherine herself.

Empress at last at the age of 33, Elisabeth quickly sought to solidify her power by choosing an heir. She had reason to believe that she would not be able to have children of her own, probably because she had conducted numerous affairs with no sign of becoming pregnant as a result. She was enormously devoted to the memory of her older sister Anne, who had married a German prince and died shortly after the birth of her son. This son, Charles Peter Ulrich, now fourteen years old, was thus sent for. Now known as the Grand Duke Peter, he was approaching his sixteenth birthday. Eager to see him married to a suitable bride, Elisabeth had turned to the family of her beloved, prematurely deceased fiancé; specifically, to the woman who would have been her sister-in-law, Johanna, Princess of Anhalt-Zerbst, who had a young daughter about the grand duke's age.

Chapter Two: Grand Duchess Ekaterina

"That year [1744], Catherine II arrived with her mother in Moscow on February 9. At that time, the Russian court was divided into two large factions or parties. The leader of the first group, who had begun to recover from his weakened position, was Vice-Chancellor Bestuzhev-Ryumin. He was infinitely more feared than loved, exceedingly scheming, suspicious, willful, and daring, rather tyrannical in his principles, an implacable enemy, but a friend to his friends, whom he abandoned only when they turned their backs on him, and often overly exacting. He was in charge of the department of foreign affairs. Having battled with the Empress's entourage, he had lost ground before the journey to Moscow, but had begun to recover. He supported the courts of Vienna, Saxony, and England. The arrival of Catherine II and her mother gave him no pleasure. It was the secret work of the faction opposed to him. The enemies of Count Bestuzhev were numerous, but he made them all tremble. He had the advantage over them in his position and his character, which gave him immense influence in the politics of the antechamber."

from the memoirs of Catherine the Great

Peter, the intended bridegroom of Princess Sophie of Anhalt-Zerbst had led a difficult life prior to his elevation to grand duke of Imperial Russia. His mother, Anne, daughter of Peter the Great, had been a very superior sort of woman, beautiful, intelligent, and intellectually accomplished. But she had died when he was very small, leaving him in the care of his father, who took little notice of him. His father, Charles Frederick, Duke of Holstein, was the son of the sister of Charles XII of Sweden. He had lived in hope of succeeding to the Swedish throne when the old king died, but when he was passed over for this honor, he presented himself at the court of Peter the Great, Sweden's greatest military rival. There, Charles Frederick was welcomed and accepted, and there, he met and married Peter's daughter. The couple returned to Holstein after the death of Catherine I, and after Anne's death, little Charles Peter was given over to the care of tutors and a French governess. Though the boy was not so intellectually inclined as his mother, he showed an early, moderate aptitude for languages, and an affinity for music that was not encouraged.

Disaster struck Charles Peter's life when his father died. Though he played only a small role in his son's upbringing, Charles Frederick had, at least, not been unkind towards him. But after his father's death, he was given over to the guardianship of his uncle, Prince Adolphus Frederick of Holstein, the Lutheran Prince-Bishop of Lübeck, who was even more neglectful than Charles Frederick had been. Rather than supervising the boy's education personally, he placed him in the care of a sadistic military officer named Otto Brümmer, the very man who would one day pen the letter that summoned Johanna Elisabeth of Anhalt-Zerbst to come to Russia with her daughter.

Considering that Charles Peter was now the Duke of Holstein in his own right, and that he was the presumptive heir to the throne of Sweden as well as a possible heir to the throne of Russia, one would think that self-interest, if nothing else, would have made Brümmer kind, eager to earn the gratitude and love of a future monarch. Instead, Brümmer was nothing less than brutal, viciously abusive even by the standards of 18th century child-rearing norms. Charles Peter was prone to sickness, was delicate in his build, and although he was military-mad, he wasn't strong enough for a soldier's life. For some reason, Brümmer responded to this frailty by beating the child with sticks and riding crops, making him kneel on dried peas, mocking and humiliating him publicly, and starving him. If Charles Peter's academic performance did not please his tutors, Brümmer would scream at him during dinner until he was so frightened that he vomited, and the next day, as punishment for the mess, he would be forced to "stand by the door at mealtimes with a picture of a donkey hung around his neck, watching his own courtiers eat".

Thus it was that by the time Elisabeth summoned her beloved sister's son to her court in Russia, the grand duke's character had been irretrievably twisted by the cruel treatment he had received. He could not fight back against his abuser, so he vented his rage on servants and small animals. He was temperamental, cringing, untruthful, desperate for someone to trust but incapable of believing in anyone's loyalty. Though Elisabeth was determined to love him for her sister's sake, she knew nothing of Brümmer's character, and he was permitted to remain close by as a member of Peter's household. Unsurprisingly, under such strain, Peter made no improvement. He was miserable in Russia and desperately homesick. He did not want to learn the Russian language or Russian history, geography, or culture; in short, he was destined to rule a country that, to him, was no better than a prison. Elisabeth saw with despair how little progress her nephew was making with his instructors, but she had no choice save to proceed with her plans and invest him as her heir. After a torturous effort, Peter learned enough Orthodox theology to make a formal, public conversion, after which he was elevated to the status of grand duke and became an Imperial Highness. Elisabeth had her heir, but he required something extra, something to make him grow up and embrace his new responsibilities. He was only fifteen, but a wife, Elisabeth thought, might do the trick. Thus the urgency that was evident in the letter she sent to Johanna, Princess of Anhalt-Zerbst, the woman who ought to have been her sister-in-law. A German bride was needed for the grand duke who was still German in all but name. If anything could help him to feel more at home, perhaps it was that.

Princess Sophie meets Grand Duke Peter

Princess Sophie and her mother arrived in Moscow in early February of 1744. They reached the city early in the day, but were asked to postpone their arrival at the palace until after dark. While they were waiting for the Empress to make her first appearance, the grand duke rushed out to greet them, claiming that he could not wait any longer before he spoke to them. He was in high spirits, chattering nervously, bounding across the room, scarcely allowing Sophie or her mother to get a word in edgewise. Sophie was struck by how little her cousin had changed since last she saw him, though more than three years had passed. He was still thin and sickly, his complexion white and his long blonde hair stringy. It was evident that he had not matured much, physically or emotionally, and was far more a child in temperament than Sophie, though she was a year younger than he.

Catherine the Great's memoirs contain a recollection of her first ten days in the presence of her Imperial cousin and his aunt, the Empress.

"The grand duke appeared to rejoice at the arrival of my mother and myself. I was in my fifteenth year. During the first ten days he paid me much attention. Even then and in that short time, I saw and understood that he did not care much for the nation that he was destined to rule, and that he clung to Lutheranism, did not like his entourage, and was very childish. I remained silent and listened, and this gained me his trust. I remember him telling me that among other things, what pleased him most about me was that I was his second cousin, and that because I was related to him, he could speak to me with an open heart. Then he told me that he was in love with one of the Empress's maids of honor, who had been dismissed from the court because of the misfortune of her mother, one Madame Lopukhina, who had been exiled to Siberia, that he would have liked to marry her, but that he was resigned to marry me because his aunt desired it. I listened with a blush to these family confidences, thanking him for his ready trust, but deep in my heart I was astonished by his imprudence and lack of judgment in many matters."

Though the grand duke did not make a promising impression on Sophie, Sophie made an excellent first impression upon Elisabeth, who found her intelligent, modest, and attractive. She invested Johanna and Sophie both with the Order of St. Catherine and appointed them to lavish apartments, with such rich furnishings that a delighted Johanna wrote to her husband that they were being treated like queens. It was quickly apparent to Sophie that her position in the Russian court depended entirely upon Elisabeth's goodwill, and that it was her favor, even more than Peter's, which she must court if the marriage was to take place as planned. She had two crucial tasks: she must learn Russian (Peter had made very little progress in his language lessons and could barely make himself understood in that language, to Elisabeth's distress) and she must make a formal study of the Orthodox rite and make a formal conversion as soon as possible (Peter had accomplished this, but only with the help of round-the-clock nagging and tutoring.) Elisabeth sent instructors in language and religion to Sophie, and she devoted herself to continuous study.

Illness

Ironically, it was Sophie's dedication to her studies which nearly ended her promising career as soon as it began. One night, staying up late to read by candlelight, she caught a chill which turned into a bad cold. Elisabeth was away from court on retreat at a nearby monastery, and Sophie was entirely under the authority of her careless mother, who refused to treat her illness as seriously as it deserved. Sophie developed pneumonia and pleurisy as a result. Only then did Johanna realize the danger, but she immediately came into conflict with Elisabeth's court physicians. In the 18th century, bloodletting was considered the most effective treatment for any severe illness; disease was thought to reside in the blood, and by drawing moderate quantities of blood from the patient, it was thought that the damaging effects of the infection could be lessened. But Johanna believed that Sophie had smallpox, and her brother had died in Russia after coming down with smallpox and being treated with repeated bloodlettings. She adamantly refused to let the doctors perform the treatment until Elisabeth received word of Sophie's illness and returned to the palace. Furious with Johanna, Elisabeth banished her from Sophie's rooms and nursed her personally until she was better. She came very close to dying, and when she was recovered, she realized that the atmosphere of the court had changed in a pointed way. As she writes in her memoirs:

"I perceived immediately that my mother's conduct during my illness had done her a disservice in the opinion of all. When she saw me gravely ill, she wanted a Lutheran pastor brought to me. I was told that I was awakened and this was proposed to me, and that I replied: 'What is the use, send instead for Simeon Theodorsky [her Orthodox spiritual instructor]; I will be happy to talk with him.' He was brought to me and he spoke to me in the presence of the attendants in a way that pleased everyone. This act gained me great favor in the opinion of the Empress and of the entire court. Another small affair further undermined my mother. Around Easter, one morning my mother decided to send a chambermaid to tell me to give her a blue-and-silver cloth that my father's brother had given me when I left for Russia, because I liked the cloth very much. I sent word to her that she was free to take it, that it was true that I liked it very much because my uncle had given it to me knowing that it pleased me. My entourage, seeing that I gave the cloth against my will and that I had been between life and death for so long and only recently had begun to improve, said to one another that it was quite imprudent of my mother to cause a dying child the least displeasure, and that far from wanting to acquire this cloth, she would have done better not to mention it. This incident was recounted to the Empress, who immediately sent me several superb pieces of rich cloth, including a blue-and-silver one. But the incident hurt my mother in her esteem. My mother was accused of having neither tenderness nor concern for me."

Though the tone of this passage is objective and dispassionate, it can only be supposed that Sophie was struck by the difference between the treatment she received from Elisabeth and her ladies of the court and the treatment she had always been accustomed to receiving from her mother. Elisabeth stayed by her side continually for an entire month, stroking her hair and holding her the way that a mother would, though her own mother had only snapped at her when she groaned in pain. More importantly, Sophie's own behavior—her quiet patience, her preference for an Orthodox confessor over a Lutheran minister, the fact that she had become ill because of her desire to learn Russian—had won the hearts of all who observed her. As a newcomer to the court, a foreigner and a German, destined to marry the unpopular grand duke who made no secret of his contempt for the country he would one day rule, Sophie had been regarded with a certain amount of suspicion. But now, as news spread of her courage and her dedication to her new homeland, she was beginning to be beloved by her future subjects. Though she could not have known this, she was already paving the way towards a time when she would be a much loved ruler of Russia in her own right.

The Bestuzhev incident

Johanna was in precisely the opposite situation. She had never treated Sophie as anything more than a means to further her own ambition, and at every opportunity she had put herself forward at her daughter's expense. Back home, where she was the wife of a sovereign prince, she could get away with this. But here in Russia, it was Sophie who mattered, Sophie on whom the hopes of the Empress depended. Johanna was always destined to take second place to a daughter who, after her marriage, would outrank her, but she had no one but herself and her own bad behavior to blame for making herself unpopular.

Johanna, driven by what can only be regarded as a narcissistic rage, made life as difficult for her daughter she could get away with following Sophie's illness. Peter, too, soon earned Johanna's enmity; he, like her, was immature, petty, and quick to take offense, though at least he had the excuse of his age. Duty-bound to be obedient to her mother and pleasing to her future husband, Sophie was placed in an impossible position.

Johanna's grandiose delusions of her own importance took a near-fatal turn shortly after Sophie recovered from her bout with pneumonia. She had not forgotten the task with which she had been entrusted by Frederick II. But the Prussian king, who had taken pains to study the character of the young princess through whom he hoped to make a permanent alliance with Russia, had not troubled to take an equally exacting character of his undercover ambassador. In short, he had commissioned Johanna to perform a task that required subtlety, delicacy, and intelligence—qualities which she simply did not possess.

Forewarned that Elisabeth's vice chancellor, Count Bestuzhev, would do everything in his power to prevent Sophie's marriage to Peter, Johanna had lost no time in allying herself with his rivals, the Prussian and French ambassadors. They exchanged secret letters conspiring to destroy his career, but their plotting was amateurish and they uncovered nothing of substance that could be used against him. Johanna was particularly indiscreet in her correspondence, making insulting comments about the Empress's appearance and personal habits. Unbeknownst to any of the conspirators, Bestuzhev was aware of the plot against them, and had been secretly intercepting, decoding, and copying their letters almost from the time of Johanna's arrival in Moscow. Bestuzhev bided his time until he had collected almost fifty incriminating letters before he showed them to the Empress; Elisabeth's fury was epic. Sophie had no knowledge of the affair until the day that Elisabeth came to their apartments to confront her mother. She heard angry voices shouting in the next room, and eventually Elisabeth emerged, red-faced, and her mother followed, weeping inconsolably. Sophie quickly stepped forward and bowed to Elisabeth, who paused and smiled at her, as if to show that her anger with Johanna did not extend to her.

Johanna had done precisely the opposite of what Frederick had wished; far from promoting Prussian interests at the Russian court, Johanna had guaranteed that, within the year, his ambassador would be dismissed and sent home. Furthermore, she had scuttled her chances of ever being anything more than her daughter's chaperone; Elisabeth was now determined that Johanna should leave Russia as soon as Sophie was married.

Conversion and betrothal

Sophie could not be formally betrothed to the grand duke until she had made her conversion to the Orthodox faith. Though she had studied faithfully with her tutor and made an intense study of Orthodox doctrine, the prospect of abandoning the strict Lutheran principles with which she had been raised caused her some disquiet. She wanted her father's approval, having promised him that she would remain faithful to her religious upbringing, but he was slow to give it; Frederick II was forced to send a special religious representative to Christian August to explain to him that the Orthodox and Lutheran faiths were not so very different in essentials before he would give his formal consent.

On June 28, 1744, Sophie entered the Orthodox church, accompanied by Elisabeth, where she delivered a long confession, written in Russian, which she had memorized. It was at this moment that she traded the name she had been given at birth for the name by which she would be known to history: Ekaterina, or Catherine. Elisabeth had requested that she not be re-baptized as Sophia, because Peter the Great's half-sister, who had led rebellions against him, had been named Sophia. Catherine, however, had been the name under which Elisabeth's mother had ruled as empress.

The day after the ceremony, on June 29, the newly baptized Catherine presented herself at the Kremlin for her betrothal to the Grand Duke Peter. The ceremony was four hours long, a grueling ordeal for Johanna, who did not take kindly to the realization that she was now, officially, a step below her daughter in matters of rank and precedence. Though Elisabeth took pains to distinguish Johanna with her notice during the ceremony, despite the antipathy which had grown between them, Johanna became furious when she realized that she could not be seated at the Empress's table, because it was reserved for Imperial Highnesses only. A private table had to be arranged for her, so that she was not forced to take her place amongst Elisabeth's ladies-in-waiting.

The marriage could not take place immediately, much to Elisabeth's distress, because Peter's doctors were not certain whether he had reached puberty, and doubted that he was capable of fathering a child. In the mean time, Elisabeth organized a pilgrimage to Kiev, to solidify Catherine's new position as a daughter of the Orthodox church. Tensions erupted during the journey as a result of Johanna's resentment towards Catherine's new rank and her growing dislike of the grand duke. During the pilgrimage, while they were staying in the town of Koseletz, an incident occurred which highlighted the strained relations between Johanna and her future son-in-law. Catherine writes in her memoirs that:

"One day the grand duke entered our room while my mother was writing and had her writing case open next to her, and he wanted to rummage in it out of curiosity. My mother told him not to touch it, and he actually went jumping across the room away from her, but in jumping here and there to make me laugh, he caught the lid of the open case and knocked it over. At this my mother grew angry and there were heated words between them. My mother reproached him for having upset the case deliberately, while he decried her injustice, and both appealed to me, demanding my corroboration. Knowing my mother's temper, I was afraid of being slapped if I did not agree with her, and wanting neither to lie nor offend the grand duke, I found myself caught in the cross fire. Nevertheless, I told my mother that I did not think that the Grand duke had done it intentionally, but that his robe had caught the cover of the case, which had been placed on a very small stool. Then my mother took me to task because when she was upset, she needed someone to quarrel with. I fell silent and began to cry. The grand duke, seeing that all my mother's anger fell on me because I had spoken in his favor and because I cried, accused my mother of injustice and excessive fury, while she told him that he was an ill-bred little boy. In a word, it would have been impossible to take the quarrel further without coming to blows, which neither of them did, however. From this moment, the grand duke took a great dislike to my mother and never forgot this quarrel; for her part, my mother also held a grudge against him, and their interaction with each other became awkward and distrustful with a tendency towards bitterness. Both of them could barely hide this from me. As hard as I worked to mollify them both, I succeeded only for brief moments. Each always had some sarcastic barb ready to sting the other. My situation grew thornier each day as a result. I strove to obey the one and please the other, and in truth, at that time the grand duke bared his heart to me more than to anyone else, and he saw that my mother often scolded me when she could not quarrel with him. This did not hurt me in his esteem, because he felt he could trust me."

Cathcrinc had yet another difficult personality to manage: Elisabeth, though fond of her, was beginning to grow jealous of her. Catherine's looks had improved greatly since she first came to Russia, and her popularity at court was increasing every day. Catherine, unlike her mother, was not in the least vain; she wanted more than anything to make everyone like her, knowing that her position as a foreign outsider in the Russian court depended on cultivating goodwill as widely as possible. She cultivated alliances for practical reasons of safety and security, rather than to hear herself being praised. She desired no one's favor as much as Elisabeth's, on whom so much depended, but she was shortly to learn that Elisabeth, for all her better qualities, had a monstrous ego, and was susceptible to abrupt changes of mood. On one awkward occasion, when Elisabeth, Catherine, and Peter were attending the opera, Elisabeth sent her French ambassador to Catherine's box in the middle of the performance to inform her of a grievance:

"One day when my mother and I were at the theater with the grand duke in a loge across from that of Her Imperial Majesty, I noticed that the Empress was speaking quite heatedly and angrily with Count Lestocq. When she had finished, Monsieur Lestocq left her and came to our loge. He approached me and said, 'Did you see how the Empress was speaking to me?' I said yes. 'Well,' he said, 'she is quite angry with you.' 'With me? Why?' was my response. 'Because,' he said, 'you have many debts. She says that one can empty wells and that when she was a princess, she had no more support than you have and an entire household to maintain and that she was careful not to indebt herself because she knew that no one would pay for her.'

Catherine, stunned by this sudden outburst of recrimination, which could certainly have waited until after the performance was over, immediately requested the record of her personal accounts and found that she had exceeded the income given to her by the Empress by about 2000 rubles—an extremely small sum compared to how much the Empress spent on trifles every day. Catherine had no extravagant personal habits, but she had sent money to her father to assist with medical treatment for her younger brother. Furthermore, she had noticed that the fastest way to make people like her—her fiancé and her mother, primarily—was to give them expensive presents. And lastly, because her mother had not furnished her with a single new dress prior to her arrival in Russia, and because the fashions of the court required ladies to change their outfits four or five times a day, she had been forced to purchase a new wardrobe. There was little to be done about these necessary expenses, or about Elisabeth's changeable moods. Like her mother's ill humor and her fiancé's childishness, Catherine would simply have to bear it until a change in circumstances gave her some relief.

Smallpox

Catherine's relationship with her future husband took a sharp turn for the worse in February of 1745, when the grand duke was afflicted, first with measles, then with smallpox. At first, his life was despaired of, and Catherine immediately noticed a change in how she was treated by members of the court. Her status depended entirely on the assumption that she would one day be the wife of the tsar; once it was assumed that he could not survive, there was nothing for anyone to gain from paying any attention to Catherine. She was not permitted to visit him because she had never had smallpox, and thus had no immunity, but in her concern for Peter's health she wrote a number of anxious letters to the Empress, who was nursing him personally, as she had nursed Catherine during her illness. She even made the effort of writing these letters in Russian, which she was still learning, with the help of her tutor; unbeknownst to her, Elisabeth found this gesture particularly touching.

Catherine was relieved when Peter was declared to be out of danger and lost no time visiting him. But no one had warned her that the smallpox had changed his appearance drastically, for the worse. In her memoirs, she writes of seeing him again for the first time, a meeting that took place in a dimly lit hall, so as to soften the sight of his disfigurement:

"At the beginning of February the Empress returned with the grand duke... As soon as we were told that she had arrived, we were to greet her and met her in the great hall between four and five in the evening, more or less in darkness. Despite this I was almost frightened to see the grand duke, who had grown a great deal but whose physiognomy was unrecognizable. All of his features were enlarged, his face was still completely swollen, and one saw that he would doubtless be quite scarred. As his hair had been cut, he wore an immense wig that disfigured him all the more. He approached me and asked if I found it hard to recognize him. I stammered my congratulations on his recovery, but in truth he had become hideous."

The long, dangerous illness Peter had suffered, and the changes to his physical appearance, took an enormous toll on him mentally and emotionally, as well as physically. Already unbalanced after years of abuse at the hands of his tutor, he had started to trust Catherine, less as future wife and more as a playmate and friendly cousin. But even though he had never played the role of a lover towards Catherine, it distressed him to realize, as he must have realized, that he was now physically repellant to her. He did not possess the emotional maturity to cope with this change in their relationship; he began to withdraw his trust and confidence from Catherine, and she, not understanding why his attitude towards her had changed so abruptly, mirrored his coolness and distance.

By contrast, Elisabeth became all the more affectionate towards the girl she referred to as her niece. She must have been concerned, on some level at least, that Catherine would wish to end her betrothal now that her fiancé was ugly, and she tried to compensate for this by securing Catherine to herself with even stronger bonds of affection. In truth, Catherine had no intention of attempting to extricate herself from the upcoming marriage. She had never been in love with Peter, or felt physical attraction towards him; she was determined to marry him because she wanted to be empress of Russia one day, and his appearance, however unattractively altered, made no difference to her in that regard.

Marriage

It had been a year since Catherine arrived in Russia, and during that time both she and her intended bridegroom had suffered near fatal illnesses. Once Peter had recovered from his bout with smallpox, Elisabeth could no longer restrain her impatience for the wedding to take place. The sooner Catherine and Peter produced an heir, the sooner the succession, and thus the future of the country, would be secured. Thus, in March of 1745, one month after Peter was declared to be out of danger, Elisabeth announced that the wedding would take place in the summer of that year. The intervening months would be devoted to elaborate preparations for an immense celebration that would prove Russia's wealth and stability to the world.

The marriage took place without any unpleasant setbacks, although Catherine was unhappy that her father was not invited. Elisabeth did not explain her reasons for this, and Catherine didn't dare ask, but it was an intentional slight against Johanna, who was by now so far out of Elisabeth's favor that she was hardly seen at court anymore.

The real problem arose immediately after the wedding was concluded. Elisabeth was so impatient for the young couple to settle down to the business of producing an heir that she excused them from the wedding ball only half an hour after it had begun. Catherine was whisked away by her maids, dressed in a French nightgown, and put to bed to await her new husband. Hours passed and he did not arrive. Finally, at midnight, he stumbled into their bedchamber, drunk from a long supper with his servants, and fell asleep immediately. The fact was, neither Catherine nor Peter had been given the slightest instruction in what we would call sex ed. The night before her wedding, Catherine confessed that she did not even know the first details of male physiognomy, and when she asked her mother to enlighten her, Johanna reprimanded her for asking such a crude question. She, like Catherine, had been fifteen when she was married, and no one had prepared her for the realities of married life, either.

Peter was allowed to repine in similar ignorance. He spent his days in his private chambers with his servants, dressing them up in uniforms and putting them through drills; Elisabeth had given her military-mad nephew a commission in a regiment when he first arrived in Russia, but Peter had sneered at the uniforms and trappings of the Russian military, so different from the crisp tailoring of Prussian soldiers from his homeland. His servants provided him with his only instructions about marriage, but they were simultaneously crude and vague. All he retained from their lessons was that a husband had the right of absolute authority over his wife, that no real man would allow his wife to have an opinion that differed from his, and that physical violence was sometimes necessary to enforce this hierarchy. This pleased Peter, who had always found relief from the pressures of his existence by hurting weaker creatures, and he made certain to explain the oppressive advice he had received to Catherine in great detail.

The first, sexless night of their marriage set the tone for the next nine years: it took that long for the marriage to be consummated. Less than a month after the wedding, Peter informed his new bride that he was in love with one of the ladies of the court. Catherine writes of her reaction in her memoirs:

"I would have been ready to like my new husband had he been capable of affection or willing to show any. But in the very first days of our marriage, I came to a sad conclusion about him. I

50

said to myself, 'If you allow yourself to love that man, you will be the unhappiest creature on this earth. With your temperament, you will expect some response whereas this man scarcely looks at you, talks of nothing but dolls, and pays more attention to any other woman than yourself. You are too proud to complain, therefore, attention, please, and keep on a leash any affection you might feel for this gentleman; you have yourself to think about, my dear girl.' This first scar made upon my impressionable heart remained with me forever; never did this firm resolution leave my head; but I took good care not to tell anybody that I had resolved never to love without restraint a man who would not return this love in full; such was my disposition that my heart would have belonged entirely and without reserve to a husband who loved only me."

Chapter Three: Marriage and Motherhood

Jealousies at court

Catherine made an unwelcome discovery very shortly after she was married: the Empress, after taking such pains to win her affection and loyalty, had a very different attitude towards her once the ties between their families had been irrevocably solemnized by matrimony. Before the marriage, it was necessary for Elisabeth to keep in Catherine's good graces, at least to a certain extent; now that Johanna had been sent back to her family and husband in Zerbst, and Catherine was left alone in Russia with a husband who ignored and despised her, Elisabeth became controlling. Catherine endured a bewildering incident in the first weeks after her marriage in which Elisabeth summarily dismissed Maria Zhukova, Catherine's favorite lady-in-waiting, and sent her out of the city with her family. Even her brother, a regimental officer, had been transferred away from the palace. The only reason given was that Catherine had become too fond of the girl. Catherine, dismayed by the fact that Zhukova was suffering for no greater crime than winning her affection, arranged a marriage between her and a prosperous officer in the Imperial Guards. But when Elisabeth learned of the marriage, she had the girl's new husband transferred to a remote rural posting.

The only conclusion Catherine could draw from this was that Elisabeth was sending a message to the entire court: no one was to get too close to the Grand Duchess or the Grand Duke without her explicit approval. Too much depended on them for the Empress to allow them to direct their own affairs. It is even possible that Elisabeth blamed Catherine's friendship with Maria Zhukova for the fact that Catherine did not become pregnant immediately after the wedding. Whether this was because she suspected a romantic connection between the two girls, or whether she merely thought that Catherine was turning to her friends for the emotional consolation she ought to have been seeking from her husband, there is no way of knowing.

The young court

By May of 1746, Elisabeth was growing suspicious of the fact that Catherine had not yet produced an heir, and for guidance, she turned to her vice-chancellor, Count Bestuzhev. He recommended that Catherine be assigned a governess, a woman whose duty

"...would be to superintend the marital intimacies and ensure the fidelity of Catherine and Peter. She was to watch the grand duchess and prevent any familiarity with the cavaliers, pages, and servants of the court. Further, she was to see that her charge wrote no letters and had no private conversations with anyone. This prohibition neatly combined Elizabeth's worries about infidelity with Bestuzhev's insistence on political isolation [from Prussian elements at court]; it was critically important to the chancellor that Catherine's correspondence and her conversations with foreign diplomats be kept under strict surveillance. Thus, Bestuzhev imposed a new entourage on Catherine, charged to enforce a new set of rules dictated by the chancellor, supposedly aimed at consolidating the mutual affection of the married couple, but also intended to render them politically harmless."

The woman selected to execute this duty was Maria Choglokova. She was twenty-four, a member of Elisabeth's mother's family, and, in Catherine's own words, "simple-minded, uneducated, cruel, malicious, capricious, and self-serving." She would act as Elisabeth's proxy to control Catherine for the next seven years. Her husband, who was no better than herself, was appointed to be Peter's governor. Peter had dismissed the vicious Otto Brümmer and sent him back to Holstein the moment he came of age, but Choglokov was not much better than Brümmer. Catherine described him as "an arrogant, brutal fool; a stupid, conceited, malicious, pompous, secretive and silent man who never smiled; a man to be despised as well as feared." This was again the doing of Bestuzhev, who believed that the daughter of the woman who had begun conspiring against him from the moment she arrived in Russia must be a conspirator herself.

Because the Choglokovs acted together to prevent Peter or Catherine from speaking in private with a single soul, servant or courtier, they could only talk to one another. This was Elizabeth's plan from the beginning; she hoped to force them into each other's arms. Catherine writes:

"In his distress, the grand duke, deprived of everyone suspected of being attached to him, and being unable to open his heart to anyone else, turned to me. He often came to my room. He felt that I was the only person with whom he could talk without every word being turned into a crime. I realized his position and was sorry for him and tried to offer all the consolation in my power. Actually, I would often be exhausted by these visits which lasted several hours because he never sat down and I had to walk up and down the room with him all the time. He walked fast and took great strides so that it was difficult to keep up with him and at the same time to continue a conversation about very specialized military details about which he spoke interminably. I knew that it was the only amusement he had."

The Choglokovs continued to dominate the "young court", as Peter and Catherine's household was called, without challenge, until Monsieur Choglokov was discovered to have impregnated one of the servants. After much pleading, the Empress forgave him and permitted him to continue in his duties, but neither he nor his wife dared be quite so severe as before. In the mean time, a Madame Praskovia Vladislavova was assigned to Catherine's household. Catherine described her as "a living archive...from her, I learned more about what had happened in Russia over the past hundred years than anywhere else. When I was bored, I got her talking which she was always ready to do. I discovered that she often disapproved of the Choglokovs, both their words and deeds. On the other hand, because Madame Vladislavova often went to the empress's apartments and nobody knew why, everyone remained wary." In this way, Catherine's boredom and confinement were eased, slightly.

Sergei Saltykov

Over the course of the next five years, Catherine and Peter's life kept to a fairly mundane course of balls, closely monitored outings, and forced intimacy between the married couple. Catherine was obliged to nurse her husband's fragile emotional equilibrium, to give way to his opinions and please him in all things, though he took no interest in anything that gave her pleasure and did not reciprocate her services as a confidante. Catherine was bored and stifled, unable to speak her mind or form friendships or pursue her interests openly. Sometimes she managed to sneak her pastimes under the noses of her observers, such as when she went horseback riding. Catherine was a superb horsewoman, and though she was forbidden to ride astride because Elisabeth believed that this practice made women incapable of becoming pregnant, she designed and commissioned a special saddle with a moveable pommel which she could convert from a side saddle to a traditional saddle as soon as she had ridden a short way from the stables.

Catherine grew daily in health and beauty, and she began to attract devoted male admirers. Everyone knew that she and the grand duke did not practice marital relations, and Catherine was mortified by the fact that Peter's rejection of her was common knowledge. But in the eyes of many men, this was all the more reason to pay her compliments and attempt to get into her good graces—if she was lonely, then she was all the more likely to be susceptible to their attentions. One of these admirers was none other than the odious Monsieur Choglokov himself, and when Catherine repeatedly and politely spurned his every attention, her relationship with the grateful Madame Choglokova improved slightly. Other admirers included Alexis Razumovsky, the younger brother of the man who, for many years, had been the Empress's common law husband. Catherine was not so repelled by Razumovsky as she was by Choglokov, but she did not encourage the attentions of any of her admirers. Though she was undoubtedly lonely, her primary goal was always to get along in the Imperial court as best she could and do nothing that would rouse the Empress's ire.

Then, in September of 1751, Catherine met the Saltykov brothers, Peter and Sergei, young noblemen assigned to the grand duke's household by Elisabeth. The elder brother, Peter, did not win Catherine's admiration; she described him as a fool with a stupid face, overly fond of gossip. Sergei, the younger brother, met with a very different reception. Biographer of Catherine the Great, Robert Massie, describes Sergei Saltykov as follows:

"Sergei was handsome and ruthless: a man who was making the seduction of women his life's purpose. He was dark-complexioned, with black eyes, of medium height, and muscular yet graceful. Constantly on the lookout for a new triumph, he always went straight to work, employing charm, promises, and persistence, in whatever combination worked."

Sergei Saltykov was already married when he joined the grand duke's household and met Catherine. His love of conquest meant that the difficulties of paying court to a closely observed Imperial bride only increased his ardor. He noticed that she was neglected by her husband, and the rumors that she was still a virgin made her all the more enticing an object for seduction. Catherine noticed that he was frequently near her, and that he was making a particular point of insinuating himself into the good graces of the Choglokovs; since, Catherine knew very well, the Choglokovs were stupid, boring, and narrow-minded, there was no reason for him to pay them these attentions. He must have an ulterior motive. In her memoirs, she gives no indication that she had figured out the nature of this motive until the moment he declared himself to her, but it seems improbable that she had not already guessed. She describes the moment of revelation thus:

"During [a concert], Sergei Saltykov intimated to me the reason for his frequent appearances. At first I did not respond. When he spoke to me about it again, I asked him what he hoped to gain. He began to paint a picture as cheerful as it was passionate of the happiness he expected. I said, 'And your wife, whom you married for love two years ago and with whom you are said to be madly in love, and she with you, what would she say?' He told me that all that glittered was not gold, and that he was paying dearly for a moment of blindness. I did everything I could to make him change his mind. I truly believed that I was succeeding. I pitied him. But to my misfortune, I listened to him. He was remarkably handsome, and surely no one equaled him in the grand court, much less in ours. He lacked neither intelligence, nor that breadth of knowledge, manners, and tact that high society, but especially the court, provides. He was twenty-six years old. All in all, he was both by his birth and by several other qualities a distinguished gentleman. He knew how to hide his faults, the greatest of which were a mind for intrigue and lack of principles; at the time, these were not yet evident to me. I held out during the spring and part of the summer. I saw him almost every day. I did not change my conduct with him at all. I was as I had always been with him and as I was with everyone else. I saw him only in the presence of the court. One day, to get rid of him for good, I decided to tell him that his attentions were in vain. I added, 'For all you know, my heart may belong to another.'

"Sergei Saltykov waited for the moment when [we were alone] and approached me to speak of his favorite subject. I listened to him more patiently than usual. He described in detail the plan that he had devised to shroud in complete secrecy, so he said, the pleasures that one could enjoy in such a situation. I did not say a word. He took advantage of my silence to persuade me that he loved me passionately, and he begged me to allow him to believe that he could hope, and that at least I was not indifferent to him. I told him that he could give rein to his imagination without me being able to prevent him... After an hour and a half of conversation, I told him to go because such a long conversation could become suspicious. He told me that he would not go unless I told him that he was tolerated. I replied, 'Yes, yes, but go away.' He said, 'I take you at your word,' and spurred his horse, and I cried, 'No, no,' and he repeated, 'Yes, yes.'"

When Catherine and Saltykov began their affair in September of 1752, a year after they first met, Peter seemed to know about it immediately. But in keeping with his behavior towards Catherine since they first met, in which he professed to be in love with other women and encouraged Catherine to flirt with other men, he seemed not to mind in the slightest—rather, he took pleasure from the fact that the whole thing was happening under the nose of Choglokov, who was still acting as his minder, and still under the impression that Saltykov considered him a close friend.

That summer, Elisabeth was informed by Madame Choglokova that the young couple had never been sexually intimate. Elisabeth had been informed of this fact before but had always been reluctant to believe it. But with the information coming from the very person she had assigned to watch Catherine's every move, she found it difficult to remain in denial. She told Madame Choglokova that she must find a way to bring the consummation about, and Choglokova resorted to a direct strategy: she sought around for a respectable, but socially inferior woman who was attractive and sexually experienced, preferably a widow, to initiate the recalcitrant and juvenile grand duke into sexual knowledge.

This task accomplished, Choglokova turned next to Catherine:

"Meanwhile, Madame Choglokova, who always had her favorite project in mind, which was to ensure the succession, took me aside one day and said, 'Listen, I must speak to you very seriously.' I kept my eyes and ears open as one might expect. She began with a long disquisition, as was her wont, about her devotion to her husband, about her virtue, about what must and must not be done to love each other and to promote or support conjugal bonds, and then she pushed on, saying that there were sometimes situations of major consequence that should be exceptions to the rule. I let her say everything she wanted without interrupting, not knowing where she was going with this, a bit astonished, and not knowing if she was setting a trap for me or if she spoke sincerely. As I was having these private reflections, she said, 'You are going to see how much I love my country and how sincere I am. I do not doubt that you fancy someone. You are free to choose between S.S. [Sergei Saltykov] and L.N. [Lev Naryshkin, another gentleman of the grand duke's household]. If I am not mistaken, it is the latter.' At this I cried out, 'No, no, not at all.' Then she said, 'Well then, if it is not him, it is the other no doubt.' I did not say a word, and she continued, 'You will see that I will not make difficulties for you.' I played dumb to the point where she scolded me many times, both in the city and eventually in the country, where we went after Easter."

One can imagine how stunned Catherine was at finding herself drawn into this conversation. For months she had been contemplating conducting an affair with Sergei Saltykov under conditions of the utmost secrecy, terrified that being discovered would lead to her ruin. Suddenly, the very person whom she most feared being found out by was authorizing, even demanding that the affair take place. Catherine can be forgiven for wondering if it was a trap.

However, Catherine, being aware that Elisabeth's attitudes towards sexual morality were, in some ways, less than conventional, might have correctly perceived that Madame Choglokova's proposition was in keeping with the Empress's desires. Elisabeth herself had freely pursued relationships with lovers all her adult life—there was no reason not to, after her fiancé died, because her predecessor, Empress Anna, would not allow her to make another political match. Elisabeth believed that God had made her beautiful for a reason, and if that reason was not to make an illustrious marriage, then it was to enjoy all the pleasures of love. Catherine was at least somewhat aware of this, so it may have seemed to her that Madame Choglokova's advice was not so terribly strange after all.

Birth

Peter and Catherine were now both aware of what husbands and wives must do in order to produce children, but it isn't clear whether this immediately led to the assumption of marital relations between them. However, in December of 1752, Catherine suffered a miscarriage after a long, sleigh journey of several days; she had a second miscarriage in June of the following year, during which her life was in serious danger for almost two weeks. At last, in February of 1754, Catherine became pregnant for a third time, and on September 20, 1754, she gave birth to a baby boy. The moment the baby was born, Elisabeth, who had been waiting in the room, whisked him away for a week. She named him Paul, after her own older brother who had died as a child. Catherine was left to lie on a pallet on the floor after the birth, and for three hours her own attendants would not help her move to the bed or give her any water without permission of the midwife, who was with the Empress.

Catherine's relationship with her son would be troubled throughout the rest of her life. During his infancy she was never allowed to spend time alone with him, never allowed to hold him or be present for the milestones of his development. The treatment she received after his birth proved to her that she had never been more than a vehicle for delivering an heir to the Empress, who effectively seized the child as state property and took it upon herself to act as the baby's mother. It was traditional for highborn women, like Catherine, to receive fabulous presents from their family upon the birth of a child, particularly a firstborn son. From Peter, naturally, Catherine received nothing, and the Empress's gifts were paltry. Elisabeth sent her a necklace and a pair of earrings worth less than one hundred rubles, and a bank draft for one hundred thousand rubles, which Elisabeth's ministers requested that she return almost as soon as it was given to her. The reason for this was that the grand duke had been incensed that Catherine had been given a gift of money when no such gift had been offered to him; the Empress instantly ordered that the same sum be given to him, but the Imperial treasury did not have enough funds to cover the order, so Catherine's gift was in effect transferred to her husband, who did not share a penny of it.

Catherine was forced to remain alone in confinement for another few weeks, during which she was left entirely to herself to cope with boredom and depression. Her lover, Sergei Saltykov, was unable to visit, because Catherine had been moved to a suite of rooms within the Empress's chamber. Then, shortly after the birth, Elisabeth made Saltykov her envoy to announce Paul's birth to the court of the king of Sweden, a journey of such distance that it effectively put an end to his affair with Catherine. She had noticed that his affections were waning in any case. Once their affair received the semi-official sanction of Madame Choglokova, the spark was gone for him. Saltykov was motivated by the desire to make conquests; once the difficulties and danger of the affair were done away with, he lost interest.

When Saltykov reached Sweden, he found that his affair with Catherine was an open secret there, and that people treated him as the father of the future heir to the Russian throne. There has been much speculation throughout history that Saltykov, not the grand duke, was in fact the father of baby Paul.

Catherine herself believed this was likely the case. Yet, portraits of the adult emperor Paul I reveal a strong resemblance between himself and Peter, and no particular resemblance to Saltykov, whom Catherine once described as being "handsome as the dawn". Paul did not even especially resemble Catherine. In his portraits, the Habsburg mouth, the rounded face, and peculiar squashed nose are all reminiscent of Peter III.

Catherine's transformation

Throughout her memoirs, which were written after she had become empress, Catherine refers consistently to the ambition which shaped her behavior during her first decade in Russia. She was dedicated to the goal of marrying the grand duke and remaining in the Empress's favor for one reason and one reason only: she meant, one day, to be Empress of Russia, not as consort, but as supreme ruler. Whether she truly anticipated, when still a teenager, that she would one day occupy the throne, or whether she was interpreting the actions of her younger self from the perspective of one who had already achieved that destiny, the period immediately following Paul's birth was one of preparation for the challenges of ruling. She was left almost entirely to herself once she had discharged the duty of delivering an heir. Having no friendly company or amusing occupations with which to divert herself, she began reading. Catherine had always been a great reader, and from her childhood she had been instilled with the necessary discipline for self-directed scholarship, but previously she had preferred to read romances. Now she dedicated herself to a course of reading that included the great French political philosophers, Montesquieu and Voltaire, as well as the *Annals* of Tacitus.

When Catherine finally emerged from this period of isolation, it was with the awareness that she had a new basis of power to draw upon. While her marriage to Peter remained unconsummated and childless, there was always the possibility that she could be cast aside—Peter the Great had divorced his first wife and confined her to a convent for the rest of her life. But as the mother of the heir to Russia, Catherine had a new official status that could not be contravened. Elisabeth's immediate predecessor had been Anna of Courland, a mother acting as regent for her infant son. Even though Elisabeth had essentially absconded with the baby, so long as Paul was a young child, Catherine, as his mother, had genuine political status. And now that she had been isolated from all her friends and close connections at court, she decided to capitalize on this status. She was to begin by transforming her image at court from that of a docile, dutiful, meek dependent, to that of a mature woman who remembered all the suffering she had been made to endure—suffering she was not disposed to forgive.

Even before Paul's birth, Catherine had begun to consolidate her power base by reconciling with the man who had authorized the Choglokovs to act as autocrats in the young court—Count Bestuzhev himself. She had sent him a message indicating that she was willing to let bygones be bygones, and he had surprised her by his enthusiastic response. What Bestuzhev had learned after almost a decade of receiving reports from his spies regarding the Grand Duke and Duchess was that Peter was weak, suffering from a case of arrested development, a drunkard whose only amusement in life was playing with toy soldiers and memorizing military protocol he would never make use of. Catherine, by contrast, was highly intelligent, discreet, and self-disciplined. Furthermore, Peter was still in love with his native Holstein and cared nothing at all for the country he was meant to rule. Catherine, by contrast, had devoted herself to the care and study of her adopted country. In this she was the precise opposite of her mother, whose foolish attempts to involve herself in international politics had motivated Bestuzhev to place such a close watch on her in the first place. Bestuzhev's position was no longer as secure as it had been when Catherine first came to court; a new favorite, Ivan Shuvalov, had supplanted him in Elisabeth's esteem. Furthermore, Elisabeth was now in her mid-forties, and had begun to have trouble with her health. Bestuzhev had to anticipate the day when the Prussian-oriented Peter might take the throne and undo all of the vice-chancellor's work in opposing the influence of Frederick II. The capable and Russian-oriented Catherine he now saw as an indispensable future ally.

Ivan Shuvalov and his wife were enemies that Catherine and Bestuzhev had in common. The Shuvalovs had replaced the Choglokovs as the governors of the "young court", and while Catherine had gradually come to win the Choglokovs over and make friends with them, she despised the Shuvalovs. She began her campaign to transform her image in the court during her first public appearance after Paul's birth, on Peter's birthday. At the ball, she dispensed with her customarily docile and diplomatic manner and criticized the Shuvalovs before an appreciative audience of courtiers. The Shuvalovs were so powerful that no one but the mother of the new heir could publicly oppose them, and they had made many enemies, who were only too delighted to see Catherine sneer at their ignorance and hypocrisy. Catherine writes that:

"For this day [the birthday celebration] I had made a superb outfit of blue velvet embroidered in gold. As I had had much time for reflection in my solitude, I resolved to make those who had caused me so many sorrows understand that they were answerable to me, that no one mistreated me with impunity, and that cruel conduct would not gain my affection or approbation. Consequently I never failed to show the Shuvalovs how they had disposed me in their favor. I treated them with bitter scorn, I made others aware of their nastiness, their stupidity, I ridiculed thcm, and everywhere I could, I always had some barb to throw at them, which would then race through the city, and provide malicious amusement at their expense. In a word, I avenged myself on them in every manner I could devise. In their presence I never failed to praise those whom they disliked. As there were a great many people who hated them, I did not lack for loyal allies. The Counts Razumovsky [the Empress's former lover and his brother, who had been supplanted by Ivan Shuvalov], whom I had always loved, were more flattered than ever. I redoubled my compliments and politeness toward everyone except the Shuvalovs. In a word, I drew myself up and walked with my head high, more like the leader of a very large faction than a humiliated or oppressed person. The Shuvalovs never knew on which foot to dance. They huddled together and resorted to courtiers' ruses and intrigues."

Ivan Shuvalov retaliated by ordering Peter to control his wife, but this only demonstrates how little understanding he had of their marital dynamic. Catherine had always done everything in her power to appease Peter, but it was to Catherine that Peter turned when he could not make his servants obey them. Baffled, he had wondered why it was that his servants would obey Catherine with only a word when they would not listen to him even when he beat them. He was not remotely equipped to force Catherine to do anything she did not want to do if she was ready to openly defy him, as he discovered when he attempted to carry out Shuvalov's instructions:

"To this end, one day after we had lunch, His Imperial Highness came into my room and told me that I was becoming intolerably haughty and that he knew how to bring me back to my senses. I asked him what he meant by haughty. He told me that I held myself very erect. I asked him if to please him, one had to keep one's back bent like some great master's slave. He grew angry and told me that he well knew how to bring me back to my senses. And I asked him, how? At this he put his back against the wall and drew his sword halfway out and showed it to me. I asked if this meant he wished to fight me. In that case, I would need one too. [NB: Peter had made Catherine participate in his play military drills so often that she later said she knew how to handle weapons as well as any young officer.] He put his half-drawn sword back into its scabbard and told me that I had become dreadfully nasty. I asked in, 'In what way?' He stammered, 'Well, with the Shuvalovs.' I replied that this was only recrimination and that he would do well not to speak of what he did not know or understand. He continued, 'You see what happens when you do not trust your true friends— you regret it. If you had trusted me, you would have benefited.' I said to him, 'But trust you how?' Then he began to say things that were so extravagant and nonsensical that I, seeing that he talked nonsense pure and simple, let him speak without responding and exploited what seemed to me an auspicious pause to advise him to go to bed because I saw clearly that wine had addled his reason and completely stupefied any common sense. He followed my advice and went to bed."

The same day as this incident occurred, Alexander Shuvalov, Ivan's brother, came to Catherine with one of those absurd decrees from the Empress of which there had been so many, the only purpose of which was to exert control over Catherine. He told her that the Empress had drawn up a list of various kinds of laces and ribbons that the ladies of the court were no longer allowed to wear. His true purpose, apparently, was to discover whether there was any change in Catherine's manner towards him since Peter fulfilled his orders to bring her to heel. He quickly discovered that there had not:

"To show him how His Imperial Highness had chastened me, I laughed in his face and told him he could have dispensed with notifying me of this decree because I never wore any ribbons or lace that displeased Her Imperial Majesty, that besides, I did not make beauty or finery the source of my merit, for when one was gone, the other became ridiculous, and only character endured. He listened to the end, twitching his right eye as was his habit, and left with his usual grimace. I pointed this out to those who were playing with me by imitating him, which made the group laugh."

From then on, though Catherine was never cruel to her husband and continued to give him advice and assistance when he asked for it, he began to distance himself from her. Though it seems impossible that Peter could not have always been aware that Catherine was his superior in every way, she had played the dutiful wife for so long that her sudden transformation into a confident, authoritative woman who was unwilling to humor his attempted displays of dominance seems to have shaken him.

Chapter Four: Seizing the Throne

Stanislaus Poniatowski

"She was twenty-five, that perfect moment when a woman who has any claim to beauty is at her loveliest. She had black hair, a complexion of dazzling whiteness, large, round, blue, expressive eyes, long, dark eyelashes, a Grecian nose, a mouth that seemed to ask for kisses, perfect shoulders, arms, and hands, a tall, slim figure, and a bearing which was graceful, supple, and yet of the most dignified nobility, a soft and agreeable voice, and a laugh as merry as her temperament. One moment she would be reveling in the wildest and most childish of games; a little later she would be seated at her desk, coping with the most complicated affairs of finance and politics."

This description of Catherine as she appeared in 1755 was penned by her second lover, the Polish nobleman Stanislaus Poniatowski, who had arrived in Moscow as the personal secretary of the British ambassador, Sir Charles Hanbury-Williams. Sir Charles had seized upon Catherine immediately as his sole ally in the Russian court. King George II of England had sent him to Russia to secure a treaty of defense that would bring Russian troops to the electorate of Hanover in case of attack by France or Prussia. The Empress refused to discuss matters of state with him, and the ambassador quickly perceived that Peter was intensely loyal to Prussia. Only Catherine was willing to talk with him intelligently and sensibly, and for this, he rewarded her with a line of credit to a British bank, and subtly encouraged Poniatowski, who fervently admired her beauty and intelligence, to pursue an affair with her. Poniatowski was a sober, high-minded young man three years Catherine's junior, and he was still a virgin when they met. It took several months after their first introduction for the affair to commence, but, as he writes, from the moment he first glimpsed her waiting for him in her bedchamber, "my whole life was devoted to her." He would be the father of Catherine's second child, a daughter who died after fifteen months, and as Empress, she would see to it that he became king of Poland.

Ukase

By the summer of 1756, the Empress Elisabeth was ill more often than she was healthy. Her ministers and advisors began considering the likely future of the government under the rule of Emperor Peter. No one was more alarmed by the prospect of installing this poorly educated, susceptible and weak-willed young man in the seat of power than Count Bestuzhev. As an inveterate enemy to Frederick II, he knew he could not expect to retain power for long in the government of an emperor who regarded Frederick as his role model.

Casting about for a solution, Bestuzhev turned to the one sensible, reliable person with any power in the court: his former enemy, the Grand Duchess Catherine. To her, he made a dangerous proposal: he was drawing up a *ukase*, or Imperial decree, scheduled to take immediate effect upon the moment of Elisabeth's death. It declared that Peter and Catherine would be named co-sovereigns, so that Catherine could effectively rule the country, with Bestuzhev retaining all his current power and gathering a great deal more besides; effectively, he would be shadow-emperor, working through Catherine, who would rule in Peter's name. Bestuzhev, of course, did not have the legal authority to make or enforce the *ukase*, and if the existence of such a document were discovered while Elisabeth still lived, she would very likely have Bestuzhev executed, along with any of his co-conspirators.

Catherine, though flattered at the confidence he was placing in her, was too wary of being implicated in a coup if Elisabeth learned about it. She told Bestuzhev that it was still too early to be thinking along such lines, and the matter was quietly dropped. Peter had fallen into the habit of deflecting all of his duties as the Duke of Holstein onto Catherine, who conferred with his secretary twice a week and made decisions in Peter's name on all of the matters presented to her. It may perhaps have crossed her mind that when her husband was emperor, she would be assigned to look after the affairs of Russia in the same manner. And if she was to be the ruler of Russia in deed, why not also in name?

On February 14, 1758, Bestuzhev was arrested on orders from Elisabeth, spurred on by Ivan Shuvalov and others, who were jealous of his influence. Catherine was in a state of mortal dread until Bestuzhev managed to get word to her that he had managed to burn all of his important papers, including the *ukase* that implicated her. Catherine, alarmed that she would be targeted in the purge led by Shuvalov, burned all of her own personal papers, including correspondence, notes on her reading, and essays she had written as a young girl.

The end of the affair

Poniatowski was recalled to Poland in 1758, after an excruciatingly embarrassing incident that brought his affair with Catherine to public notice. Peter was having an affair with one of Catherine's maids of honor, Elizabeth Vorontsova; Catherine was not fond of Vorontsova, whom she regarded as coarse, stupid, and ill-mannered, and Vorontsova was no better disposed towards Catherine, because her duties as Catherine's maid of honor sometimes prevented her from spending time with Peter. Unfortunately for Catherine, this spiteful enemy was in a position to know all about her affair with Poniatowski, and she likewise recognized the costume Poniatowski wore to slip in and out of the palace at night on his way to see Catherine.

Poniatowski had been recalled by the Polish court in the summer of 1758, but he was resisting his orders by feigning illness so that he could remain with Catherine. But on his way out of the palace one night in July, while he was in disguise as a tailor, he crossed paths with a carriage that Peter and his mistress were riding in. Vorontsova pointed Poniatowski out to Peter, who ordered him to halt. Never before had Peter expressed any interest or concern in Catherine's affairs with other men, but on this occasion, he asked Poniatowski directly whether he was sleeping with his, Peter's, wife. Poniatowski attempted to deny it, but Peter ordered him arrested. Realizing that the whole business was about to come out, Poniatowski asked Shuvalov to help him get back to Poland quickly to avoid an international incident, and Shuvalov agreed.

But then, something intensely peculiar occurred: Peter invited Poniatowski to visit him. He behaved in a friendly manner towards his wife's lover and invited him to have dinner with himself and his mistress, Elizabeth Vorontsova. After they had settled in around the table, and were making agreeable conversation, Peter abruptly declared that someone was missing from the party. He dashed off to Catherine's room, scarcely giving her time to put on a robe over her night gown, and brought her in to be seated with the others. Neither Poniatowski nor Catherine knew what to make of this. Peter appeared to be enjoying himself immensely, as if satisfied that he had managed to discomfit his superior wife for once. Catherine, however, found the whole affair distasteful. Poniatowski left for Poland within a few days; it was the end of his affair with Catherine, but not the end of their friendship. Years later, when Poniatowski had been named king in Poland due to Catherine's influence, he set down his impressions of Peter, by then long dead:

"Nature made him a mere poltroon, a guzzler, an individual comic in all things. In one of those outpourings of his heart to me, he observed, 'See how unhappy I am. If I had only entered into the service of the King of Prussia I would have served him to the best of my ability. By this present time, I should, I am confident, have had a regiment and the rank of major general and perhaps even of lieutenant general. But far from it. Instead, they brought me here and made me a grand duke of this damned country.' And then he railed against the Russian nation in his familiar, low, burlesque style, yet at times really very agreeably, because he did not lack a certain kind of spirit. He was not stupid, but mad, and as he loved to drink, this helped scramble his poor brains even further."

The Death of Empress Elisabeth

As Elisabeth's health showed signs of failing rapidly—she had a stroke and collapsed in public on the way out of church, which meant that her health problems could no longer be concealed from the public—Catherine's mind turned again to her political future. There were three options before her: either Peter would put her aside, as he had been threatening to do, so that he could marry his mistress, Elizabeth Vorontsova, or Peter might keep her on so that she could perform the same administrative functions in the rule of the empire that she was already performing in Peter's rule of Holstein. Or some means might be found to exclude Peter from the line of succession so that the throne might pass to the seven year old Paul instead, with Catherine acting as his regent. Privately, Catherine was contemplating a fourth option—replacing Peter in the line of succession herself, with Paul as her heir rather than her emperor-in-waiting. But this ambition she kept to herself for the time being.

Others in Elisabeth's court were also looking to the future, with Catherine as their surest bet for stability in the times to come. Ivan Shuvalov, Elisabeth's favorite and Catherine's chief enemy at court, was one of those who approached her in private, hoping to win her trust; he hoped to serve the same function for her that he had served for Elisabeth. But Catherine had a new lover, Gregory Orlov, a famous soldier of the Imperial Guard whose father had won favor and renown under Peter the Great. By August of 1761, Catherine was pregnant with his child. Orlov had four brothers who were also enormously popular officers in the Guards, and they looked upon the affair approvingly. By taking their youngest brother to her bed, they considered that Catherine had done their family a great honor. Furthermore, Peter's contempt for Russian soldiers was well known, as was the fact that Catherine's sympathies, despite her German birth, were entirely Russian. She became the natural object of their loyalty.

Catherine had another ally in the form of Princess Catherine Dashkova, whose maiden name was Vorontsova; she was the sister of Elizabeth Vorontsova, Peter's mistress. Peter also happened to be Dashkova's godfather. Unlike her coarse, ignorant older sister, Catherine Dashkova was well educated, fluent in French and Italian, and she shared Catherine's fondness for reading French philosophers. Catherine had never met a woman in the Russian court with whom she could speak of the interests that were closest to her heart, and she went out of her way to show favor to the younger girl. Dashkova was devoted to Catherine as a consequence. Dashkova's husband, Prince Michael Dashkov, was an officer in the Preobrazhensky Guards, the regiment formed by Peter the Great which had marched at the Empress Elisabeth's back when she seized the throne from Anna of Courland. In the summer of 1761, Catherine took to calling on Dashkova daily during her visits to watch her son Paul playing in the gardens. During these visits, they discussed political theory, and Dashkova became convinced that Catherine, not Peter, must be the next ruler of Russia.

Peter, who was fond of Dashkova for her older sister's sake, actually tried to play the role of a concerned godfather with her, one of the few duties in his life he may have taken seriously. He was concerned by her obvious idolatry of Catherine, and advised her, saying, "My child, you would do well to remember that it is much safer to deal with honest blockheads like your sister and me than with those great wits who squeeze the juice out of the orange and then throw away the rind." But the more time Dashkova spent in the presence of her sister and her sister's lover, the more determined she was to support Catherine in all things. She began to repeat to Catherine all that she heard Peter and Vorontsova saying about her in private, including Peter's increasingly bold hints that he meant to divorce Catherine as soon as he was crowned and discontinue the war against Prussia.

Anticipating his elevation to the throne, Peter was already doing all that he could to assist Frederick II, and though he made no secret of the fact that he was committing acts that in any lesser person would be punishable as treason, no one was willing to take measures to stop him, for fear that he would retaliate when he was emperor. But Peter's contempt for the Russian soldiery meant that he was blind and deaf to the army's growing hatred of him. The five Orlov brothers in particular were incensed against the grand duke. Gregory Orlov, whose love for Catherine was absolute, was frightened of what might become of her once Peter had the authority to do as he liked. He and his brothers began to spread the word amongst their fellow soldiers in the Imperial Guards, and in the other regiments: the grand duchess was the victim of her foolish husband's shameful neglect, she was a faithful daughter of the Orthodox church, she had taken it upon herself to learn the culture and language of the Russian people, and from the moment of her arrival in the country she had done everything in her power to uphold Russian interests. Unbeknownst to the grand duke, or even to Catherine herself, the Orlov brothers were inciting the army to discard their loyalty to the Imperial heir and transfer their allegiance to a worthier object.

By late December of 1761, Elisabeth was very near to her death. She had been virtually incapacitated by illness for months, but she had concealed this information from the public. Catherine likewise was six months pregnant by Gregory Orlov, but she too had managed to keep this a strict secret—even her husband and intimate friends did not know. On December 20, five days before Elisabeth's death, Peter told Catherine Dashkova that he had absolutely resolved to put Catherine aside and marry her sister. Dashkova, who was ill with fever, crept from her bed in the middle of the night and stole in secret to the palace where Catherine was sleeping and told her everything.

On December 23, 1761, the Empress suffered a stroke. She died forty-eight hours later, on Christmas Day, surrounded by Peter, Catherine, her lovers Ivan Shuvalov and Alexis Razumovsky, and a few others. She was lucid to the end, and Peter was terrified that she might still deprive him of the throne, which she was legally capable of doing simply by uttering the word in the presence of witnesses. She did not do so, however, and as soon as Elisabeth, daughter of Peter the Great, drew her last breath, the Grand Duke Peter was named Emperor Peter III.

The seven-month reign of Peter III

Contrary to the fears of most reasonable people, the early days of the new emperor's short reign were not an immediate disaster. Though he had no fixed philosophy of government, his initial acts were of a moderate bent. He won popularity by lowering the state tax on salt, and by releasing the landowning classes from Peter the Great's policy of compulsory government service.

However, Peter III made two disastrous missteps that fatally eroded his budding popularity: he attacked, first the Russian church then the Russian army. Peter was a Lutheran at heart, so when he attempted a reform of the Orthodox church, it was to make it more European and more Protestant. He ordered that all church property was to be secularized, that is, assumed by the state, and that the clergy were to be considered employees of the Imperial government and receive state salaries. More distressingly for the Russian people, and in keeping with the Protestant view that icons were no better than idols, he ordered that all icons of Russian saints were to be removed from the churches; only icons of Christ were permitted to remain. Furthermore, Orthodox priests were ordered to shave their beards, and exchange their long, embroidered robes for the simple black robes worn by Protestant clerics. Traditional Russian religious celebrations, like the outdoor Easter processions, were banned.

As to the army, Peter was determined to break it down and build it back up again along Prussian lines. The traditional uniforms of the Russian army, which included long, loose-fitting coats that insulated soldiers against the Russian winter, were to be traded for the trim, tailored blue uniforms worn by Prussian soldiers. The games Peter had played for years in his private chambers, drilling his servants like a regiment of soldiers, were transferred to the parade ground, as the historic regiments of the Russian army were forced to conduct Prussian style drills. He dismissed the emperor's traditional guard, composed of the best soldiers of the Preobrazhensky Regiment, and instated a regiment of soldiers from Holstein as his bodyguards. What feelings this aroused in soldiers like Gregory Orlov can well be imagined.

The new emperor erred even more disastrously when it came to ending Russia's role in the Seven Years' war. On her deathbed, the Empress Elisabeth had prosecuted the war against Prussia with all that remained of her energy. By the time she died, Frederick II, once commander of the mightiest and largest army on earth, had lost all but 3000 of his men. Ill with rheumatism, Frederick was weak and depleted in resources, and his surrender was imminent—until Peter III took the throne. The new emperor immediately "declared peace", abandoned Russia's alliances with France and Austria, and began the process of using Russia's resources to extricate Prussia from ruin. As historian Robert Massie puts it:

"This sensational diplomatic and military *volte-face* startled the chancelleries of Europe. When Maria Theresa's government in Vienna learned that the Russian emperor meant to sacrifice all his conquests 'in the name of peace', the Austrian reply was guarded, asking for details as to how this was to be achieved. The Russian explanation, arriving in April, was pretentious and pompous: to make peace, it declared, one belligerent must step forward as a general proponent and agent of peace; Russia had chosen this role 'out of compassion for suffering humanity and from personal friendship for the king of Prussia. The Austrian court is therefore invited to follow our example.' To Vienna, this message was menacing; the threat became real when Peter signed the treaty of alliance with Frederick. Peter explained this by saying that inasmuch as his good offices had proved useless, he found himself regretfully compelled to resort to the extreme measure of assisting the king of Prussia with his army as being the quickest way to restore to humanity the blessings of peace."

No sooner had Peter effectively forced Austria and France into a compromise deal with Prussia, he was making war with Denmark on behalf of Holstein. Frederick II wrote urgently to Peter, advising him that he should not over-extend himself so early in his reign. He had not yet been formally crowned, but he was proposing to place himself at the head of an army and venture on a risky military exercise hundreds of miles from the seat of his throne. Frederick sensed the possibility of a coup and attempted to warn Peter of this possibility. But Peter wrote back that he felt perfectly safe in Russia. He ordered 40,000 Russian troops to the border of Pomerania, intending to meet them and take his place as their commander. He never got the opportunity, however; before he could set out, he had been captured, imprisoned, and deposed.

A new empress

"It does not appear that the empress is much consulted," wrote the British ambassador in his reports to London regarding the court of the new emperor. "The empress bears the emperor's conduct and the arrogance of Vorontsova nobly," reported the French ambassador, saying that Catherine put a "manly face on her troubles; she is as much loved and respect as the emperor is despised."

By the spring of 1762, Catherine knew her days as empress were numbered. Peter paraded his mistress openly at state banquets and before dignitaries. He even contrived to humiliate Catherine publicly by ordering her to bestow the Order of St. Catherine upon Elizabeth Vorontsova, the same honor which the Empress Elisabeth had conferred upon Catherine when she first arrived in Russia, an honor that was meant to be reserved for empresses and grand duchesses. But there was little Catherine could do either to defend herself or change the situation; she was exhausted and physically encumbered by her pregnancy, which was approaching its end. Her son, Alexis Gregorovich, who would later become Count Bobrinsky, was born on April 11; during the birth, Catherine was attended by no one save her midwife, and as soon as the infant had been delivered he was immediately conveyed to the home of her loyal valet, to be nursed by his wife.

Matters came to a head between Peter and Catherine during a state banquet the following month. Toasts were offered to the Imperial family; Catherine kept her seat as the guests drank to her health. Peter, feeling that Catherine ought to have joined in the toast as a mark of respect for his two uncles from Holstein, shouted at her before all the assembled guests, calling her a fool. Later that night, he ordered her arrested. The order was countermanded when the commander in chief of the Russian army intervened on Catherine's behalf. This was Prince George Lewis of Holstein, a man with no military experience, who had been placed in charge of the army by Peter simply because he was Prussian and a relative. Prince George also happened to be Catherine's uncle; Peter knew this, but he did not know that the prince had once been in love with Catherine and had asked her to marry him when she was only fourteen. Prince George pointed out to the emperor that by imprisoning Catherine he risked turning the army against him. Peter capitulated, but when news reached Catherine of her narrow escape, she realized that the moment had come to act. If she did not depose Peter now, she risked losing everything. Always before, she had demurred when those around her proposed placing her on the throne in Peter's stead. Now she was prepared to give these plans her open cooperation.

On June 19, 1762, Peter and Catherine saw each other for the last time. Peter had made all necessary preparations to depart for Denmark at the head of his military campaign, and he celebrated by attending an opera that evening, where he played the violin with the backing of the orchestra. Catherine was in attendance. Unbeknownst to him, she had also been making preparations. The Orlovs had been gaining the support of over fifty officers in the various guard regiments, dispensing gifts of wine and money in her name. The Swedish ambassador, Panin, had been entrusted by Catherine with guarding her son Paul. Panin was also the head of the Russian Academy of Sciences, where he had ordered the printing of a document that claimed that the emperor, Peter III, had chosen to voluntarily abdicate his throne in favor of his wife Catherine, with his son Paul as her heir. This pamphlet was ready to be distributed as soon as the critical moment arrived.

A week later, on June 27, one of the officers who had been gathering support for Catherine in secret was arrested. Fearing that he would be forced to confess the plot under torture, Panin and the Orlov brothers rushed into action. Originally, they had intended to arrest the emperor and hold him under guard while Catherine was proclaimed empress in the capital, but the arrest of the officer left no time for this. The Orlovs communicated to the guard regiments that the empress's life was in danger, and Alexis Orlov traveled twenty miles during the night to the palace where Catherine was staying. At five in the morning, he entered her chamber, awakening her with the words, "Matushka [little mother], wake up! The time has come! You must get up and come with me! Everything is ready for your proclamation!" He then told her of the arrest that had taken place. Catherine rose immediately and made the twenty-mile journey back to the capital with him. She was taken directly to the barracks of the Izmailovsky Guards, who received her as their sovereign, kissing her hands and the hem of her simple black dress. She explained to them that the emperor meant to kill her and her son Paul in order to replace her with Elizabeth Vorontsova. In order to preserve the supremacy of the Orthodox faith in Russia, she was thus obliged to remove the emperor from power. There, in the company of the regiment, she was proclaimed for the first time as Catherine II of Russia.

Other guard regiments quickly fell in line to support Catherine. In the city, she received a blessing from the archbishop of Novgorod and proceeded to the Winter Palace, surrounded by ebullient soldiers, cheering crowds, and the sounds of church bells ringing. Panin, former ambassador to the Swedish court, came to join her, accompanied by her son Paul. Catherine made a critical calculation in that moment. She might have chosen to present herself to the people as the mother of the new tsar, acting as his regent; instead, lifting the seven-year-old boy up on high where the crowd could see him, she declared him to be her heir, and thus herself to be the rightful empress. Then, before the Senate and the princes of the Orthodox church, she declared that,

"...Catherine, moved by the perils threatening Russia and the Orthodox religion, eager to rescue Russia from a shameful dependence on foreign powers, and sustained by divine providence, had yielded to the clear wishes of her faithful subjects that she should ascend the throne."

In this manner, Catherine II conquered the city of St. Petersburg without shedding a single drop of blood.

There was just one problem: Peter remained in ignorance of all these events. He had not abdicated, nor been arrested, and large portions of the army still believed they owed him their loyalty. If he were to make contact with Prussia, Frederick II would undoubtedly lend him the military support he needed to raise an armed counter-rebellion. It was of paramount importance that Peter be found and persuaded to accept the new status quo without resistance.

Peter was at that time staying at Oraniebaum, a large Imperial residence west of St. Petersburg, the summer retreat built by Peter the Great. Catherine ought to have been with him—she had spent the last sixteen summers there—but he had excluded her from the trip in order to bring Elizabeth Vorontsova with him. Sovereigns of Russia were entitled to the rank of colonel in the Preobrazhensky Guards, and Catherine decided to fulfill the duties of an officer in person: dressing herself in a soldier's uniform, with a sword at her side, she mounted a white horse and set out at the head of 14,000 men and five regiments of infantry and Imperial Guards to bring Peter the bad news. The young Princess Dashkova, her adoring friend, also donned an officer's uniform and rode at her side.

Peter, meanwhile, was preparing for his name day celebrations (similar to a birthday, persons of the Orthodox faith celebrated the feast day of the saint for whom they were named; in Peter's case, the feast of St. Peter and St. Paul). He and his entourage rode to the house in Peterhof where Catherine was expected to offer him formal congratulations, but they found the house empty. Soon, rumors began trickling in of the revolt occurring in St. Petersburg in Catherine's name. Peter's Holstein guards advised him to flee instantly for Prussia, where Frederick II could ensure his life and his freedom, but Peter refused to go. He was convinced that the people of Russia preferred him to his wife; he swore to defend his throne with his life. But every attempt he made to rally the armies of Russia to his banner failed.

Not until the soldiers at the fortress of Kronstadt refused to allow him to set foot on the island, asserting that they recognized no ruler but Catherine II, did Peter admit defeat. He returned to Oraniebaum and sent away all of his advisors and attendants, apart from Elizabeth Vorontsova, who refused to leave him. There, he wrote a letter to Catherine, admitting that his behavior towards her had been wrong, and offering, pleadingly, to make her his co-ruler if she would allow it. Catherine received this letter a few hours later, but chose not to reply to it; she already was too secure in her possession of the throne to give half of it back to Peter again. When Peter realized that no reply was forthcoming, he wrote her a second letter, this time offering to abdicate his throne and return quietly to Holstein, so long as he could take Elizabeth Vorontsova with him. To this, Catherine professed herself agreeable, so long as Peter presented his abdication in writing. Peter complied, writing,

"I, Peter, of my own free will hereby solemnly declare, not only to the whole Russian empire, but also to the whole world, that I forever renounce the throne of Russia to the end of my days. Nor will I ever seek to recover the same at any time or by anybody's assistance, and I swear this before God."

It is not surprising that Catherine believed him sincere. She knew better than anyone how miserable her husband had been in Russia, how little he cared for its customs, language, religion, or people, and how devoted he was to his native Holstein. Though the humiliation of having his throne stolen from him was bitter, she was, in effect, offering to give him the very thing he had always wanted. Peter did not realize that the promises made to him would not be kept; he was shortly to part from Elizabeth Vorontsova for the last time, and he would not return to Holstein again before his death. Catherine had no desire to be cruel, but it was impossible for her to permit Peter to live within reach of Frederick II, who would undoubtedly use him to interfere in Russian affairs in the future.

Catherine's desire was to see Peter rendered harmless; but how to manage this, she was not certain. Her temporary orders were that Peter was to be incarcerated in the same fortress where the deposed tsar Ivan VI, former ward of the regent Anna of Courland, had lived his whole life. While his rooms there were being prepared, he was allowed to live in one of the Imperial summer houses of his choosing. He remained there under guard for about three days, during which time he wrote three pathetic letters to Catherine, begging her to reduce the number of soldiers who were guarding him. Anxiety had reduced him to an emotional and physical wreck, and he was so ill that doctors had to be sent for. Despite the danger that Peter posed to her while he lived, Catherine had not discussed the prospect of having him executed with any of her co-conspirators. But the Orlov brothers, aware that her reign could not be truly secure as long as Peter lived, may have been prepared to take fatal measures on her behalf and without her direct authorization. The true facts of Peter's death are unknown, but Catherine received the following letter on July 7, 1762 from Alexis Orlov, whom she had placed in charge of Peter during his imprisonment:

"Matushka, Little Mother, most merciful Gosudarina, sovereign lady, how can I explain or describe what happened? You will not believe your faithful servant, but before God I speak the truth, Matushka. I am ready for death, but I myself know not how it came about. We are lost if you do not have mercy on us. Matushka, he is no more. But no one intended it so. How could any of us have ventured to raise our hands against our Gosudar, our sovereign lord. But, Gosudarina, it has happened. At dinner, he started quarreling and struggling with Prince Bariatinsky at the table. Before we could separate them, he was dead. We ourselves know not what we did. But we are all equally guilty and deserve to die. Have mercy on me, if only for my brother's sake. I have confessed my guilt and there is nothing further for me to tell. Forgive us or quickly make an end of me. The sun will no longer shine for me and life is not worth living. We have angered you and lost our souls forever."

"My horror at this death is inexpressible," Catherine said, when she received this letter. "This blow strikes me to earth." Whatever secret thoughts she might have harbored about Peter's future as her prisoner, her distress over his death was genuine. Not only did she still feel pity for her husband, whom she had known since he was a small boy, but she was too sophisticated not to realize that all of Europe would blame her and think of her as a murderess. In this, she was correct; the courts of Europe spoke openly of her accession as a return to the days of the murderous Ivan the Terrible. But foreign monarchs such as Frederick II, who had access to better intelligence and firsthand knowledge of the people involved, understood Catherine to be blameless. Alexis Orlov and his brothers were not punished for the death; though he and his brothers were prepared to kill in Catherine's name, the frantic tone of Alexis's letter could scarcely have been faked by a man who was not accustomed to duplicity or intrigue. Catherine ordered Peter's body autopsied, and doctors who were loyal to her declared his death to be a result of natural causes. Afterwards, Catherine published the following announcement:

"On the seventh day of our reign we received the news to our great sorrow and affliction that it was God's will to end the life of the former emperor Peter III by a severe attack of hemorrhoidal colic. We have ordered his mortal remains to be taken to the Alexander Nevsky Monastery. We ask all our faithful subjects to bid farewell to his earthly remains without rancor and to offer up prayers for the salvation of his soul."

Catherine's son, Paul, believed all his life that his mother had ordered his father to be killed, and this belief contributed heavily towards the animosity he felt for her. Not until after her death, when he discovered the letter from Alexis Orlov among her papers, did he recognize his mother's innocence in his father's death.

Catherine's final verdict on Peter's death is found in a letter written to her former lover, Stanislaus Poniatowski, two weeks after the event. In it, she writes that,

"Fear had caused a diarrhea which lasted three days and ended on the fourth when he drank excessively...A hemorrhoidal colic seized him and affected his brain. For two days he was delirious and then delirium was followed by extreme exhaustion. Despite all the help the doctors could give him, he died while demanding a Lutheran priest. I feared that the officers might have poisoned him so I had him opened up, but not the slightest trace of poison was found. The stomach was quite healthy, but the lower bowels were greatly inflamed and a stroke of apoplexy carried him off. His heart was extraordinarily small and quite decayed.

"So at last God has brought everything to pass according to His designs. The whole thing is rather a miracle than a pre-arranged plan, for so many lucky coincidences could not have coincided unless God's hand had been over it all. Hatred of foreigners was the chief factor in the whole affair and Peter III passed for a foreigner."

Chapter Five: Catherine II of Russia

"She sat on the throne of Peter the Great and ruled an empire, the largest on earth. Her signature, inscribed on a decree, was law, and, if she chose, could mean life or death for any one of her twenty million subjects. She was intelligent, well read, and a shrewd judge of character. During the coup, she had shown determination and courage; once on the throne, she displayed an open mind, willingness to forgive, and a political morality founded on rationality and practical efficiency. She softened imperial presence with a sense of humor and a quick tongue; indeed, with Catherine, more than any other monarch of her day, there was always a wide latitude for humor. There was also a line not to be crossed, even by close friends."

Robert Massie, *Catherine the Great*

After the tumultuous week that saw Catherine elevated to the throne, and saw the former emperor, Peter III, dead in the care of Alexis Orlov, Catherine's most important task was to arrange her coronation. A coronation was a sacred and semi-mystical ceremony in which the ruler was consecrated by the will of God, the church, and the Russian people. Catherine badly needed the legitimacy that this ceremony could confer. She was unprecedented in the history of Russian rulers. The Romanov dynasty had been founded in the early 17th century, and each tsar had ruled under divine right until Peter the Great, in his modernizing reforms, declared that the tsar was "the first servant of the state", a secular executive who had made a sacred vow to uphold the interests of the empire. It was Peter the Great who had declared that male primogeniture was outdated, and that the emperor had the right to name any successor he pleased, consanguinity and birth order notwithstanding.

But Catherine was only a Romanov by marriage, and the previous emperor had not chosen her to succeed him; she had usurped the throne, albeit with a popular mandate, in a coup d'etat. Peter III had reigned seven months without ever bothering to organize his coronation, and this had contributed to the ease with which Catherine had unseated him. She would not make the same mistake. She would be crowned, in the ancient Russian capital of Moscow, as soon as possible. The announcement of her coronation went out the same day as the news of Peter's death was published. The coronation itself took place on September 22, 1762, at the Kremlin. The newly appointed English ambassador to her court wrote the following description of Catherine as she appeared at her coronation:

"...a woman of middle height, her glossy, chestnut-colored hair massed under the jeweled crown...She was beautiful, and the blue eyes beneath were remarkable for their brightness. The head was poised on a long neck, giving an impression of pride, and power, and will."

Many people had helped Catherine come to the throne. Those people must now be rewarded, according to the ranks, roles, and the degree of risk they had undertaken on her behalf. The problem was that the people who had assisted her all wanted a share of the glory, and their individual ideas of just how much glory they deserved did not always tally with how useful they had actually been. Some of the new empress's intimate friends, like Catherine Dashkova, saw themselves as having been essential to the coup, when they had actually played peripheral roles. And those who had truly been indispensable, like the Orlov brothers, were targets for the jealousy of those who had been less richly rewarded than they. During Catherine's coronation week, she was obliged to exile members of the Guards who, feeling that they had not received enough honor for their part in bringing Catherine to the throne, were overheard musing drunkenly that perhaps they ought to stage another coup, this time on behalf of the imprisoned emperor Ivan VI. Catherine was much beloved by her supporters, but there was a sense of entitlement amongst them, and she spent the first several years of her reign dispensing gifts, honors, and promotions just to cement loyalties that an empress of the Imperial Russian line would have considered to be hers by right.

The government of Catherine II

"This princess seems to combine every kind of ambition in her person. Everything that may add luster to her reign will have some attraction for her. Science and the arts will be encouraged to flourish in the empire, projects useful for the domestic economy will be undertaken. She will endeavor to reform the administration of justice and to invigorate the laws; but her policies will be based on Machiavellianism; and I should not be surprised if in this field she rivals the king of Prussia. She will adopt the prejudices of her entourage regarding the superiority of her power and will endeavor to win respect not by the sincerity and probity of her actions but also by an ostentatious display of her strength. Haughty as she is, she will stubbornly pursue her undertakings and will rarely retrace a false step. Cunning and falsity appear to be vices in her character; woe to him who puts too much trust in her. Love affairs may become a stumbling block to her ambition and prove fatal for her peace of mind. This passionate princess, still held in check by the fear and consciousness of internal troubles, will know no restraint once she believes herself firmly established."

Baron de Breteuil, French ambassador to the court of Catherine II

Catherine lost no time at the beginning of her reign reversing those measures of Peter III's which had so offended the army and the church. The army was recalled from Denmark, the regiments re-formed, their uniforms restored; in the case of the church, the lands and properties which had been assumed by the state were passed back into consecrated hands. Next, she turned her attention to the Russian senate. Since all governmental power in Russia issued from the hands of the sovereign, the Senate's role was merely to administrate the carrying out of laws passed down to them by Catherine. They were a cumbersome body, but loyal to Catherine. Her procurator general, that is, the man who functioned as her chief liaison to the Senate, received the following letter from her, describing the expectations she had for him:

"You must know with whom you have to deal... You will find that I have no other view than the general welfare and glory of the fatherland, and I wish for nothing but the happiness of my subjects... I am very fond of the truth, and you may tell me the truth fearlessly, and argue with me without any danger if it leads to good results in affairs. I hear that you are regarded as an honest man by all...I hope to show you by experience that people with such qualities do well at court. And I may add that I require no flattery from you, but only honest behavior and firmness in affairs."

Though Catherine was to stand by this policy of rewarding honesty and discouraging flattery throughout her reign, she was not what we would think of today as a moderate or progressive ruler. If anything, she tended to the opposite extreme. Her chief advisor during the first 18 years of her reign was Nikita Panin, who had formerly been Russia's ambassador to the court of the King of Sweden, and whom she had appointed to be the tutor of the tsarevitch Paul. While in Sweden, he had become a proponent of constitutional monarchy, that is, the system of government wherein the sovereign rules by consent of the people, or at least the aristocracy. In the first year of Catherine's reign, as her chief minister for foreign affairs, Panin proposed the formation of a kind of advisory council, populated by the heads of government departments such as the army and the navy, as well as by other high-ranking or well-informed Russian citizens. This council would share power with the empress, who would retain veto power over all its decisions.

But Catherine was opposed to any measure that would restrict her privileges as supreme autocrat. She was deeply interested in French Enlightenment philosophy, which advocated the rights of individuals, and would later be such a great admirer of the American Revolution that she ordered a bust of George Washington for her study. But she did not believe that the Russian nation could function as anything less than an autocracy. Her reasoning was that the country was too large, its' Senate too inefficient, and its population generally too ill-educated to take on the responsibility of self-government. Nothing would get done, she feared, if her power was not absolute. The European-based reforms of Peter the Great were less than a century old. The nation's economy still depended on the labor of the feudal serfs, who were bound to serve their landowning masters.

Serfs

In Russia in the 18th century, the lot of serfs was little better than that of slaves. They lived in terrible conditions, received no compensation for their labor, could be bought and sold for fairly trivial sums of money, and were forced to work as many hours as their owners wished them to work, without regard for their health. Families were broken up on a whim and young girls and boys forced into sexual servitude. Any sign of disobedience or rebellion could be punished with savage beatings; owners could not kill their serfs, but they could punish them in such a way that death was the inevitable result. There had been serf revolts under the Empress Elisabeth's rule, which were suppressed by the Russian army. These revolts were provoked by the rise in industrialization: factory and mine owners were purchasing serfs along with the brick and mortar properties they labored in and proceeding to work their human property to death. Many serfs attempted to flee into the countryside; others struck back against their masters.

In the summer of 1762, Catherine attempted to address the grievances of the industrial serfs and quell their rebellions by holding the industrial barons accountable for their inhumane actions. She abolished the practice of buying serfs as industrial labor unless the land on which they lived was also included in the purchase—this raised the value of serf labor, making it unprofitable for owners to discard human life in such a callous manner. She also decreed that the serfs were to be paid a small wage, agreed upon in advance. But this measure, though compassionate, brought disaster to the Russian economy. Industrial serfs, emboldened by their newly granted rights, began striking; factories and mines ceased production. Catherine, like Elisabeth before her, felt obliged to send the army to force the serfs back to work. At the same time, she instructed the general of the army to make an investigation of the serfs' complaints, to publicly punish anyone found guilty of excessive cruelty, and privately punish those who had ignored her commands:

"In a word, do everything you think proper for the satisfaction of the peasants; but take suitable precautions so that the peasants should not imagine that their managers will be afraid of them in the future. If you find managers guilty of great inhumanity, you may punish them publicly, but if someone has exacted more work than is right, you may punish him secretly; thus you will not give the common people grounds to lose their proper dutifulness."

Catherine was willing to take some measures to relieve the suffering of her subjects, but she likewise considered it essential to the welfare of the nation as a whole that the serfs remember their place:

"In all matters, according to the laws that have been enacted from time immemorial by the autocratic forefathers of Her Imperial Majesty and which have not been repealed, and which provide that all persons who dare to incite serfs and peasants to disobey their landlords shall be arrested and taken to the nearest government office, there to be punished forthwith as disturbers of the public tranquility, according to the laws and without leniency. And should it so happen that even after the publication of the present decree of Her Imperial Majesty any serfs and peasants should cease to give the proper obedience to their landlords . . . and should make bold to submit unlawful petitions complaining of their landlords, and especially to petition Her Imperial Majesty personally, then both those who make the complaints and those who write up the petitions shall be punished by the knout and forthwith deported to Nerchinsk to penal servitude for life and shall be counted as part of the quota of recruits which their landlords must furnish to the army. And in order that people everywhere may know of the present decree, it shall be read in all the churches on Sundays and holy days for one month after it is received and thereafter once every year during the great church festivals, lest anyone pretend ignorance."

Catherine and the Enlightenment

The serfs "must be set free"; this was the advice given to her by the French philosopher Voltaire, with whom Catherine corresponded throughout much of her reign. But it was not until 1861, under the rule of Tsar Alexander II, that serfdom in Russia would be ended—five years before the 13th Amendment would be passed in the United States, finally abolishing the last stronghold of government-sanctioned slavery in the Western world. Catherine's personal beliefs were opposed to serfdom, but like the framers of the American Constitution, she was up against hard political and economic realities. Men like Voltaire told her that it was immoral for human beings to be kept in bondage, but she knew that already; what people like Voltaire could not tell her was how to successfully liberate and enfranchise an entire class of people on whose labor the economy depended, who were considered by their owners to be subhuman.

Catherine was a great patroness of the French philosopher Diderot; when Diderot fell on hard times, Catherine purchased his entire library of books for sixteen thousand pounds, but she insisted they remain in Diderot's hands, with him acting as her librarian for an annual salary. This act of generosity made her famous throughout Europe as an enlightened monarch, a reputation which Russia, long regarded as a land of wilderness and savagery, sorely needed. In 1773, out of gratitude for her help, Diderot made the long and grueling journey to St. Petersburg to attend Catherine personally at her court. During his stay, Catherine reserved two hours a day for conversing with him.

While still a grand duchess, Catherine had proposed a measure, similar to that which the northern American states later adopted, of gradually freeing the serfs in her kingdom over several generations. Any time an estate changed hands, she suggested, all the serfs of that estate might be freed, and within a hundred years or so freedom would come to that entire class of people. Why she did not make this plan a policy during her reign is unclear, save that, in land-rich Russia, serfs were the basis of all wealth. There were so many of them that the lowest ranking aristocrats had three or four times the number of household servants of any European of comparable rank. Lacking a plan for freeing them and creating a place for them in society, Catherine instead reinforced their servile status. Under her rule, the lives of serfs improved, but only marginally.

Diderot, as well as Voltaire, wished to transform Catherine into a true Enlightenment ruler, a sovereign who might put all of their lofty political ideals into practice. But Catherine explained the difficulty with this in a note which she wrote to Diderot while he was staying with her:

"I have listened with the greatest pleasure to all the inspirations of your brilliant mind. But all your grand principles, which I understand very well, would do splendidly in books and very badly in practice. In your plans for reform, you are forgetting the difference between our two positions: you work only on paper which accepts anything, is smooth and flexible, and offers no obstacles either to your imagination or your pen, while I, poor empress, work on human skin, which is far more sensitive and touchy."

Catherine had hoped that by bringing Diderot to her court he might help her devise a practical schedule of reforms based on Enlightenment principles that could be introduced into Russian society without ruining the economy or inciting social revolt. But no such compromise between the hard social realities of Russian life and gentler, loftier philosophical ideals had been found. Diderot, however, was convinced that he had made a genuine convert of the Russian empress, and sang her praises for the rest of his life.

The *Instruction* of Catherine II

Perhaps the greatest state document produced during Catherine's reign was the *Nakaz[1]*, or *Instruction*, which biographer Robert Massie describes as "intended to be a guideline for a complete rewriting of the Russian legal code". The Russian legal code was, in fact, in desperate need of updating by the time Catherine took the throne. There had been no systematic overhauls since the current set of laws had been established under Tsar Alexis I, son of the founder of the Romanov dynasty, in 1649. The result was that new laws were continually being passed without reference to the old ones, creating hundreds of duplicated and contradictory statutes. Catherine's proposed solution was to bring to the capital representatives from all across the country, from all social classes (except the serfs) and all ethnic groups and religions, where, as the newly appointed Legislative Commission, they would be charged with drafting a complete set of new laws to govern the nation.

But Catherine was determined that these new laws should reflect more than the traditional moral wisdom of a people who were, in some areas, still steeped in a medieval mindset. She wanted modern laws, based on Enlightenment principles; but since few people in Russia had anything like Catherine's level of education or familiarity with Enlightenment philosophy, it would be up to her, as sovereign, to distill these principles of humane government into a

---

[1] See Appendix II for the complete text of the *Instructions.*

set of instructions, to guide the members of the assembly in their work.

Catherine composed her *Instruction* over a period of two and a half years, from January 1765 to July 1767. She drew on a wide range of influences, referencing John Locke, Montesquieu, and contemporary Italian legal scholar Cesare Beccaria, who advocated for criminal reform over incarceration and punishment. As the purpose of the *Instruction* was to acquaint a large number of people who had no background in legislation or philosophy with teachings they had never encountered before, Catherine employed a didactic, rather than a regal tone in the document, explaining what may have seemed like very basic principles to more highly educated people. She begins by reminding readers that "the Christian Law teaches us to do mutual Good to one another, as much as possibly we can." In a country, and indeed, an entire era, in which torture was practiced routinely, sometimes under flimsy pretexts, this was a principle that most of her readers probably needed to be reminded of.

Catherine's first draft of the *Instructions* did not meet with unilateral approval. Even her foreign minister, Nikita Panin, who was an admirer of Sweden's constitutional monarchy, feared the potential repercussions of such a liberalizing set of principles, and when she handed it over to the Russian Senate for review, they crossed out over half the document in their editorial notes. And in the end, the document did not have a particularly profound effect on the laws of the nation. But it won its author widespread fame in Europe; Voltaire was particularly proud of his patroness when the *Instruction* was banned in France as dangerous and likely to incite riots. He assured Catherine that this would only ensure that it was all the more widely read and circulated.

The call to gather a Legislative Commission went out as soon as Catherine finished drafting the *Instructions*. The Commission was comprised of a total of 564 delegates, including representatives from the central government departments, the aristocracy, property owners from the smaller towns, free peasants, and the various non-Russian ethnic tribes, including Muslims and Buddhists. Russian nobility tended to balk when asked to take an active role in government, particularly when this involved traveling to Moscow, which was why Peter the Great had instituted mandatory government service for the aristocratic classes. But Catherine attempted to make the prospect of government service attractive by attaching rewards, honors, and a salary to it. This made Commission members somewhat more willing to participate, but a number of them found it difficult to understand what, precisely, they were being asked to do. It was understood that the Legislative Commission would have no power to draft laws, that it would only be presenting a set of recommendations to the empress. The majority of the commissioners could not read, so the *Instruction* was read aloud to them. The essential philosophical principle they had to get their heads around was the idea that people ought to be free to do "anything that is not forbidden by law": in a strictly hierarchical society where everyone had a master they answered to, this was a strange, new, and somewhat unwelcome idea.

Ultimately, the Legislative Commission was unable to reconcile the competing needs of all the different social classes that were represented, and the attempt to produce a completely new Russian legal code failed. But by gathering the Commission, Catherine had established a new precedent for consulting and involving the people in the administration of the government. This would have far-reaching implications for Russian history. Because the Commission's reforming efforts had little effect, some scholars have concluded that its true purpose was merely to gratify Catherine's vanity by proving to the Western European powers that she was an intellectual cut above her autocratic predecessors. But Isabel de Madariga, a premier scholar of Catherine's reign, dismisses this idea:

"The idea that the principal purpose of such an expensive and time-consuming operation...was only to throw dust in the eyes of Western intellectuals...is difficult to accept. It was possible for Catherine to win their golden opinions by corresponding with them as she did with Voltaire; by buying Diderot's library and leaving it in his possession; by inviting d'Alembert and Beccaria to come to Russia; by appointing [the German philosopher] Grimm as her personal agent in Paris... This was sufficient evidence of Enlightenment credentials... There was no need for her to embark on an enterprise of such major and time-consuming dimensions as the Legislative Commission."

The most enduring legacy of the Legislative Commission was not, in the end, the reformation of Russian legal codes. At the beginning of the session, before anything else was done, the Commission felt it necessary to convey to the empress their gratitude for her condescension in consulting them in such a manner. This gratitude took the form of bestowing upon Catherine a new title. Catherine was slightly exasperated by this: "I brought them together to study laws, and they are busying discussing my virtues," she complained to one of her advisors. Nevertheless, she could only be flattered when the Senate voted to confer upon her the same appellation they had given to her predecessor, Peter I: henceforward, she would be known in Russia and across the world as Catherine the Great. Peter I had not become known as Peter the Great until he had been in power for over thirty years; Catherine, by contrast, had ruled for only five years.

The struggle to find a balance between maintaining the sovereign's autocratic powers—which Catherine regarded as essential to the smooth running of her vast nation—and giving the people a voice in government, increasingly an imperative as Enlightenment political philosophy swept Europe in the 18th century—did not only define Catherine's reign. There had never been a political document like the *Instruction* in European political history; it anticipated the Declaration of Independence, its nearest ideological cousin, by almost a decade. And the precedent Catherine had set in calling the people together to advise her in the administration of her duties was, in its way, revolutionary—so much so that no Russian ruler would dare attempt it again for over a hundred and fifty years. When Nicholas II, the last emperor of Russia, came to the throne in 1894, his reign was beset by these same concerns; he was invested in reserving the autocratic privilege of the sovereign, and would not bow to the popular mandate to create the Duma, the Russian parliamentary body, until 1905, twelve years before he was forced to abdicate in the Bolshevik Revolution of 1917. And by then it was too late: the rule of the Romanov dynasty was ended when he, his heir, the tsarevitch Alexis, and all the rest of his immediate family were executed by firing squad in 1918.

The Partition of Poland

As the ruler of a vast empire, Catherine, unlike her contemporary Frederick II of Prussia, was not especially motivated by the acquisition of new territories, save in one respect: Russia, traditionally, had been a landlocked country, lacking a seaport that was not covered in ice for half the year. Peter the

Great, in his military victories against Sweden, had secured the Port of Riga under Russian control, but Catherine needed a southern port that would give Russian sailors access to the Black Sea by riverway. In order to gain this access, Catherine turned her gaze to the politically unstable republic of Poland, whose king, in 1762, was terminally ill. Poland was ruled by its Diet, a weak, disunited parliamentary body composed of over one thousand nobles with a single vote each. Because the aristocratic classes were unwilling to choose a single family from amongst their number with whom to entrust the crown and a hereditary line of kingship, they chose their kings, who were often foreigners, by election, and though the king's appointment was for the term of his natural lifetime, he had little real power in the nation. This made Poland an easy target for the powerful nations that bordered it.

In 1762, King Augustus III, who had reigned since 1736, was dying; Catherine decided that the next Polish king should be sympathetic to Russian interests, and her mind turned immediately to the Polish nobleman who had once been her lover, Stanislaus Poniatowski. To this end, she sent her representative, Hermann Keyserling, to Poland with a purse of one hundred thousand rubles and instructions to buy as many votes as necessary to ensure Poniatowski's election. Thirty thousand Russian soldiers were deployed to the Russian-Polish border to reinforce Keyserling's negotiations, and Catherine turned to Fredrick II of Prussia and Maria Theresa of Austria to support her choice of candidate, lest her interference be seen as an act of warmongering against those nations. Frederick granted Catherine his cooperation in exchange for a mutual defense treaty between Russia and Prussia.

The chief obstacle to Catherine's plans for Poland was not the opposition of other nations, but the opposition of the chosen king himself. Stanislaus Poniatowski was still desperately in love with her. He had looked, upon Catherine's gaining the Russian throne, to be recalled to Russia as the Polish ambassador, so that they might once again resume their relationship. But Catherine was involved with Gregory Orlov, and she had enough difficulty keeping him in his place; he wanted to marry her, and her refusal to become his wife provoked him to public displays of jealousy that embarrassed her greatly. She could not risk upsetting Orlov further by bringing a former lover to her court. More importantly, from Catherine's perspective, there was no more ideal candidate for the Polish throne than Poniatowski, who was the nephew of the most powerful member of the Polish Russian-affiliated party. More importantly, he was poor, and in love with her. Through gifts of money, and his personal loyalty to her, she could be sure that he would use his power in Poland to support Russian interests. Poniatowski did not want to be king; he was certain that if only he and Catherine might lay eyes on one another again, all their former passion would be rekindled. But Catherine was firm in her refusals, and eventually he submitted to her directions, and took up his place at the head of the Polish government.

Poland was deeply religiously divided. The official religion of Poland was Roman Catholicism, and only Roman Catholics were permitted to hold seats in the Diet. But there were large populations of Russian Orthodox Poles in the eastern region of the country, and a significant number of Lutheran Poles in the northern region. These divisions aligned with the dominant religions of Poland's bordering nations: Russia was Orthodox, Prussia was Lutheran, and Austria was Roman Catholic. Because it was illegal in Poland for Orthodox or Lutheran believers to practice their religions openly, Polish dissidents felt a certain amount of loyalty for the foreign nations that shared their religions.

Upon the election of Stanislaw II August, as Poniatowski was known during his reign, the Polish Diet proposed a series of legal reforms that would, among other things, make the kingship of Poland hereditary, which would bring much-needed stability to the government. But Catherine, through her minister Repnin, made it a condition of her assent to these reforms that freedom of religion be exercised in Poland—Orthodox believers were to be permitted to meet in their own churches without harassment, and to be permitted to participate in the government. Frederick, by contrast, did not bother to pursue an agenda of tolerance for Lutheran believers, because it suited his purposes for northern Poles to feel divided from their government and their national allegiance.

When the ardently Catholic Diet voted to reject religious liberty, Catherine responded by having outspoken bishops arrested and by sending troops to the Diet to force a favorable vote for tolerance. But Catherine had underestimated the strength of Polish national feeling on the religious question; an anti-Russian rebellion broke out. She was obliged to send more troops, and institute a Russian occupation of Poland. This state of affairs could not last for long, however; Frederick had agreed to let Catherine interfere in the Polish election, but not to stand idly by while she annexed Poland into the Russian empire. Furthermore, Turkey, which bordered Poland, was alarmed by what they saw as Russian military excesses. An independent Poland had always stood between Turkey and Russia; a Poland which could function as a staging ground for a Russian invasion of Constantinople was intolerable. Turkey declared war; Frederick, and Prussia, remained neutral. He was to regret this when Catherine's army and navy mounted an almost uniformly successful military campaign against Turkey, cities and ports falling under Russian control almost as soon as their forces made contact.

Faced by Austrian threats to come to the aid of Turkey, which would activate Prussia's treaty requirement to join the war on Russia's side, Frederick devised a bold solution: dividing, or "partitioning" Poland into three territories, the Lutheran north for Prussia, the Orthodox east for

Russia, and the Roman Catholic south for Austria.[2] Catherine was not initially in favor of this plan; her ambassador in Poland was effectively in charge of the government, and Poland was poised to become a Russian vassal state which would open all of Turkey to Russian domination. But she came to see that such an agreement was preferable to provoking open war with Austria and its ally, France, who would support Turkey rather than allow Russia to seize the Balkans.

By May of 1771, Maria Theresa and Catherine had both consented to open negotiations surrounding Frederick's proposed plan of Polish partition. Maria Theresa was the most reluctant of the three rulers— she deeply disliked Frederick, with whom she had been at war for so long over possession of Silesia, and Catherine she held in contempt as a usurper and as a woman who had transgressed Catholic sexual morals by having open affairs with lovers. More importantly, as a devout Catholic, she naturally supported Poland as a Catholic sister-nation. But her son and co-ruler, Joseph II, was in favor of the partition plan, and eventually persuaded her to accept it. In the late spring of 1773, King Stanislaw II called for a meeting of the Diet, which voted to ratify partition. Russia gained nearly two million Orthodox subjects; Prussia, 600,000 Lutherans; Austria, close to three million Catholics. Only a small central portion of Poland remained independent and self-governing.

---

[2] See Appendix III for the full text of the joint Declaration of Partition.

Chapter Six: The Legacy of Catherine the Great

Medicine

In Catherine the Great's lifetime, medical science was in its infancy. Dangerous and ineffective medical practices, like bloodletting, were practiced contemporaneously with an advanced procedure still used today: inoculation. Smallpox was rampant in the 18th century, and its morbid and disfiguring effects terrified nobles and commoners alike. But the practice of cultivating an immunity to the disease by introducing a weak strain of the infection to the bloodstream was almost as feared as the disease itself. In the 1760's, inoculation was making slow inroads in Britain and the American colonies, but it was shunned by most of Europe. Catherine, however, was so afraid of smallpox that she was willing to take the risk of inoculating herself so that anxiety about the disease would no longer prey upon her mind. She summoned an American doctor to perform the procedure on her. When it proved successful, she had her son Paul, then 12 years old, inoculated as well. By the end of her reign, over 20 million Russians had been inoculated against smallpox, a virtual revolution in medical science at a time when most Europeans still considered the average Russian to be ignorant and savage in comparison to themselves.

Under Catherine's rule, the first medical schools were founded in Russia. European doctors were recruited and offered generous salaries and pensions to resettle in Russia and train students. In 1763, Catherine personally founded a hospital in Moscow exclusively for the use of poor women who needed a safe place to give birth; any woman of any social class might make use of it, and there was an anonymous safe-haven drop for infants whose mothers were unmarried or too ill or poor to care for them. All foundling orphans taken in by the hospital were cared for until they were mature enough to look after themselves, and all were free peasants under the law—even those whose mothers were serfs. The hospital was so successful that a new one was opened in St Petersburg, and by 1775, Catherine had decreed that foundling hospitals be built in the capital of every province, while all of the outlying counties were required by law to employ "a physician, a surgeon, two surgical assistants, two apprentices, and an apothecary." There was no similar system of medical care anywhere in Europe; Catherine's Russia led the world in medicine during her reign.

Gregory Potemkin

On the day that the young Catherine rode to Oraniebaum dressed in a male officer's uniform to arrest Peter III, she found that she had no way of carrying a sword, because the clothing supplied to her did not have a sword knot. No doubt the person in the Imperial Guards who gave her the clothing thought that, as a woman, she would have no desire to carry a weapon. Catherine disagreed, however, and from the ranks of the guards appeared a young man who presented her with his own sword knot. Catherine accepted the gift and promoted him to captain for his service and awarded him ten thousand rubles. This soldier was Gregory Potemkin, remembered today as the most illustrious figure to emerge on the national stage during Catherine's reign. In 1774, when her affair with the jealous, disgruntled Gregory Orlov came to an end, Potemkin, ten years her junior, became Catherine's lover.

Potemkin came of a family who had long been of service to the tsars of Russia. As a young man he was a brilliant and promising student of theology at the University of Moscow, but he discontinued his studies and joined the Horse Guards in 1759. He spoke a number of languages, and was an accomplished musician and devastatingly gifted mimic: he once made Catherine burst into gales of laughter by perfectly reproducing her low alto voice and German accent. In 1763, Catherine appointed Potemkin to be her liaison with the Holy Synod, the governing body of the Orthodox church, and in 1769 he was promoted to major general for his bravery in the war against Turkey. After the war, in 1774, he returned to Catherine's court, having received a congratulatory letter which made him believe that she had transferred her affections from Orlov to himself. When Catherine did not immediately invite him to her bedchamber, he departed the court and went to a monastery, where he gave every sign of intending to renounce his military career and become a monk. Catherine understood that this was nothing more than a ploy to make her fearful of losing him, but in truth, she needed his talents as an officer and a diplomat too much to take the risk that he might be serious in his new vocation. She recalled him to court, and installed him in the suite that connected with hers by a private staircase.

Catherine herself described Potemkin as "one of the greatest, most bizarre, and most entertaining eccentrics of the iron age." Potemkin was deeply jealous, not only of any other man to whom Catherine showed the slightest favor, but of her previous lovers; he confronted her with a rumor that she had taken at least fifteen men to bed in the same fashion as him, and she was sufficiently under his spell that she wrote to him a "Confession" in which she laid bare her entire romantic history, beginning with her unhappy marriage, then her officially sanctioned affair with Saltykov, her brief liaison with Poniatowski, her faithfulness toward Gregory Orlov (whom, she said, would have been her lifelong companion "had he himself not grown bored"), and a petty affair with a fourth man who had been recommended to her by her minister Panin, who had been sent away to the country with a pension. No one in her life, she said, had affected her as Potemkin affected her, and he could expect her to be faithful to him. Nonetheless, Potemkin was prone to frequent flares of jealousy, and Catherine was obliged to soothe and reassure him as though he was much younger than his 35 years. Potemkin and Catherine exchanged many letters, creating an extraordinary documentary trail that testifies to the tumultuousness of their affair. In one of these letters, Potemkin articulates the source of his jealousy:

"Allow me my precious dear to say these final words that will end our quarrel. Do not be surprised that I am uneasy about our love. Beyond the innumerable gifts you have bestowed on me, you have placed me in your heart. I want to be there alone, preferred to all former ones, since no one has so loved you as I. And since I am the work of your hands, so I desire that you should secure my place, that you should find joy in doing me good, that you should devise everything for my comfort and find therein repose from the great labors that occupy your lofty station."

Like Orlov before him, Potemkin was made uneasy by the fact that Catherine, as empress, could dismiss him at a moment's notice, as she had done to his predecessor. "We quarrel about power," she wrote to him, during a particularly troubled period of their relationship, "never about love." Like Orlov before him, he wished to secure his position in Catherine's life by marriage. The difference between Potemkin and Orlov is that Catherine might actually have gone through with a secret marriage to Potemkin. There is no documentary evidence, but Emperor Joseph II of Austria hinted to his British ambassador that a marriage had taken place, and it is possible that his intelligence network in Russia could have supplied him with accurate information. Catherine certainly addressed Potemkin as "my dear husband" in many of her letters, though this may have been a mere pet name. In any case, if a marriage did take place, it did not bring peace to their often contentious relationship. Potemkin took offense easily and quarreled with Catherine many times on flimsy pretexts. It is a sign of how much she loved him that she endured his temperamental behavior. After three years, they agreed to pursue relationships with other lovers, while maintaining their close emotional relationship.

Paul

In September of 1772, Paul, Catherine's son, turned eighteen. Mother and son had never enjoyed a close relationship. Having been whisked away from his mother by the Empress Elisabeth the moment he was delivered, never even held by her until he was several weeks old, she had not been given the chance to form an early bond with him. And through no fault of his own, Paul remained a living monument to an excruciatingly lonely, difficult, and painful period in her life: her loveless, humiliating marriage to the unstable Peter III, the almost equally humiliating affair with Sergei Saltykov, whom she believed to be Paul's true father. For Paul's part, even after

Elisabeth's death, his mother remained difficult to know. As empress, she was continually occupied by affairs of state, and he was deeply affected by rumors circulating in the court that Gregory Orlov, who was constantly at Catherine's side when Paul was a boy, had murdered his father Peter. Though unlike Peter in many respects—Catherine had taken special care with the boy's education, and he proved intelligent— he idolized the memory of the dead emperor, mimicking Peter's obsession with all things military and all things Prussian.

Paul and Catherine grew closer as he neared his coming of age. Orlov had been sent away from court, leaving emotional and physical space for him in Catherine's life. It was necessary that he marry soon, but she sought to give him more of a choice in his life's partner than she or Peter had been given; she invited a minor German princess with three daughters of suitable age to the Russian court, and indicated to Paul that he might choose the sister he liked best. His choice alighted on the middle sister, Wilhelmina von Hesse-Darmstadt. Wilhelmina, like Catherine, converted to the Russian Orthodox faith in preparation for the wedding, taking the name Natalia Alekseyevna. She and Paul were married in September of 1773. Tragically, however, she died three years later, during complications from a stillbirth. Paul was beside himself with grief, to the point that his mother feared for his health. Then, he suffered a counter-blow: Natalia's desk was searched, and it was discovered that she had been having an affair with Paul's best friend. Outraged, Paul put an end to his mourning and determined to re-marry immediately. His second bride, whom he married a mere five months after Natalia's death, was another German princess: Sophia von Württemburg, who took the Orthodox name of Maria. Within three years, Paul and Maria had produced two sons: Alexander, who would one day be Tsar Alexander I, and a younger brother, Constantine. Their marriage was a success. Catherine had succeeded in giving her son and heir the one crucial ingredient for a happy and stable life she had been denied—a marriage partner who could be his friend as well as his lover, devoted to his happiness and his interests.

Paul's relationship with Catherine, however, deteriorated in the years following his marriage. She was, not without cause, fearful that she would be deposed and Paul put on the throne in her place, and for this reason she limited his attempts to prepare for his future role as emperor by involving himself with the Russian military. Pressure to abdicate in favor of a male heir was often brought to bear on female monarchs once their sons were of age, and the pressure was all the more pointed because Paul was presumed to be a pedigree Romanov, while Catherine had never shaken off the cloud of a usurper. Paul's animosity and rebelliousness towards Catherine grew so pointed that she contemplated disinheriting him and naming the young Alexander as her heir. Paul suspected that she was thinking along these lines, and his resentment of Catherine grew all the stronger. He grew eccentric and paranoid, moody and unbalanced, which made Catherine all the more determined not to entrust the care of Russia to him before she could help it. Paul was so certain that Catherine meant to disinherit him that immediately after she died, he had all of her papers searched, fearful that a will would be found which would deprive him of his throne. As it happened, he was safe; Catherine had discussed the possibility of passing him over for Alexander with both Maria and the young Alexander himself, and both had refused to support such a plan. Unwilling to draft her daughter-in-law and grandson into a dynastic feud against their will, she had elected to maintain the status quo.

The Death of Catherine the Great

In August of 1782, Catherine unveiled a magnificent bronze statue, which still survives today, of Peter the Great on horseback at the moment of his greatest military victory. In Latin and Russia, it was inscribed, "To Peter the First, from Catherine the Second", and it stood as the empress's enduring final word on her own reign. Peter the Great had begun the modernization and Europeanization of Russia; five sovereigns and fifty years had passed, and then Catherine the Great had come to fulfill his unfinished mission. This was how Catherine saw herself: as a reformer, a patron of arts and sciences and philosophy, who, through sheer ability and force of will, had helped bridge the gap between her adopted nation and the rest of the civilized world.

Though she was prone to diseases, Catherine had enjoyed fairly good health for most of her life, but in the 1790's, when she was in her seventies, her robust constitution began to fail her. Headaches, rheumatism, and leg ulcers plagued her, but she did not allow them to interfere with her duties. As to her personal life, though she was vexed and grieved by her deteriorating relationship with her son Paul, she was close to her grandson Alexander, and in him she placed all her hopes for the future of her dynasty and the Russian monarchy.

Catherine's last public appearance was on November 4, 1796, at a supper held by some of her oldest friends, who had been faithful to her from the time she was a lonely grand duchess. The next morning, November 5, her servants discovered that she had collapsed on the floor in her private bathroom. Doctors concluded that she had probably suffered a stroke. She remained conscious, though unable to speak, until she died 36 hours later on November 6, 1796. Surrounding her bedside were the doctors, her confessor, her son Paul and his wife Maria, and her grandsons, Alexander and Nicholas.

The new emperor, Paul I, ordered that the coffin of Peter III be disinterred; he had not been buried in the traditional resting place of the Russian tsars, the Cathedral of St. Peter and St Paul, because he had never been formally crowned. But when Catherine was buried there on December 5, Paul saw to it that Peter's coffin was placed next to Catherine's. His final blow against the mother he had come to despise was to rescind the decree of Peter the Great that the emperors of Russia were empowered to choose their own heirs. From Paul's reign, until the end of the Romanov dynasty, Salic law was observed, which forbade women, or descendants of female members of the Imperial family, from succeeding to the throne.

One hundred and fifty years later, when the monarchy was overthrown in Russia, it would be, in part, because the only son of Nicholas II, the tsarevitch Alexis, was a hemophiliac who was not expected to survive to adulthood. Though Nicholas and his wife Alexandra had four healthy daughters, there was no question of transferring the succession to his eldest daughter, Olga. Instead, in a desperate attempt to preserve Alexis's health, the Imperial family placed themselves in the power of the monk Rasputin, which undermined their credibility abroad and with their own people. Catherine the Great had succeeded four empresses of Russia, but she would be the last female sovereign of that country. She was the longest-ruling monarch in Russian history; alongside Peter the Great, she is considered the most effective ruler Russia has ever known.

Other great books by Michael W. Simmons on Kindle, paperback and audio:

Elizabeth I: Legendary Queen Of England

Alexander Hamilton: First Architect Of The American Government

William Shakespeare: An Intimate Look Into The Life Of The Most Brilliant Writer In The History Of The English Language

Thomas Edison: American Inventor

Nikola Tesla: Prophet Of The Modern Technological Age

Albert Einstein: Father Of The Modern Scientific Age

Appendices

State Documents from the Reign of Catherine II of Russia

*

Appendix I:

Manifesto of Catherine II On European Immigration to Russia, 1763

(Catherine opened the borders of Russia to those in Europe who were seeking a better life after the ruinous effects of the Seven Year's War. Freedom of religion and language, exemption from taxation and military service, all tempted large numbers of German immigrants into "unsettled" portions of Russia, providing the country with economic benefits and providing Catherine with large numbers of loyal, grateful subjects.)

We, Catherine the second, by the Grace of God, Empress and Autocrat of all the Russians at Moscow, Kiev, Vladimir, Novgorod, Czarina of Kasan, Czarina of Astrachan, Czarina of Siberia, Lady of Pleskow and Grand Duchess of Smolensko, Duchess of Estonia and Livland, Carelial, Tver, Yugoria, Permia, Viatka and Bulgaria and others; Lady and Grand Duchess of Novgorod in the Netherland of Chernigov, Resan, Rostov, Yaroslav, Beloosrial, Udoria, Obdoria, Condinia, and Ruler of the entire North region and Lady of the Yurish, of the Cartalinian and Grusinian czars and the Cabardinian land, of the Cherkessian and Gorsian princes and the lady of the manor and sovereign of many others. As We are sufficiently aware of the vast extent of the lands within Our Empire, We perceive, among other things, that a considerable number of regions are still uncultivated which could easily and advantageously be made available for productive use of population and settlement. Most of the lands hold hidden in their depth an inexhaustible wealth of all kinds of precious ores and metals, and because they are well provided with forests, rivers and lakes, and located close to the sea for purpose of trade, they are also most convenient for the development and growth of many kinds of manufacturing, plants, and various installations. This induced Us to issue the manifesto which was published last Dec. 4, 1762, for the benefit of all Our loyal subjects. However, inasmuch as We made only a summary announcement of Our pleasure to the foreigners who would like to settle in Our Empire, we now issue for a better understanding of Our intention the following decree which We hereby solemnly establish and order to be carried out to the full.

I. We permit all foreigners to come into Our Empire, in order to settle in all the governments, just as each one may desire.

II. After arrival, such foreigners can report for this purpose not only to the Guardianship Chancellery established for foreigners in Our residence, but also, if more convenient, to the governor or commanding officer in one of the border-towns of the Empire.

III. Since those foreigners who would like to settle in Russia will also include some who do not have sufficient means to pay the required travel costs, they can report to our ministers in foreign courts, who will not only transport them to Russia at Our expense, but also provide them with travel money.

IV. As soon as these foreigners arrive in Our residence and report at the Guardianship Chancellery or in a border-town, they shall be required to state their true decision whether their real desire is to be enrolled in the guild of merchants or artisans, and become citizens, and in what city; or if they wish to settle on free, productive land in colonies and rural areas, to take up agriculture or some other useful occupation. Without delay, these people will be assigned to their destination, according to their own wishes and desires. From the following register* it can be seen in which regions of Our Empire free and suitable lands are still available. However, besides those listed, there are many more regions and all kinds of land where We will likewise permit people to settle, just as each one chooses for his best advantage.

V. Upon arrival in Our Empire, each foreigner who intends to become a settler and has reported to the Guardianship Chancellery or in other border-towns of Our Empire and, as already prescribed in # 4, has declared his decision, must take the oath of allegiance in accordance with his religious rite.

VI. In order that the foreigners who desire to settle in Our Empire may realize the extent of Our benevolence to their benefit and advantage, this is Our will -- :

1. We grant to all foreigners coming into Our Empire the free and unrestricted practice of their religion according to the precepts and usage of their Church. To those, however, who intend to settle not in cities but in colonies and villages on uninhabited lands we grant the freedom to build churches and bell towers, and to maintain the necessary number of priests and church servants, but not the construction of monasteries. On the other hand, everyone is hereby warned not to persuade or induce any of the Christian co-religionists living in Russia to accept or even assent to his faith or join his religious community, under pain of incurring the severest punishment of Our law. This prohibition does not apply to the various nationalities on the borders of Our Empire who are attached to the Mahometan faith. We permit and allow everyone to win them over and make them subject to the Christian religion in a decent way.

2. None of the foreigners who have come to settle in Russia shall be required to pay the slightest taxes to Our treasury, nor be forced to render regular or extraordinary services, nor to billet troops. Indeed, everybody shall be exempt from all taxes and tribute in the following manner: those who have been settled as colonists with their families in hitherto uninhabited regions will enjoy 30 years of exemption; those who have established themselves, at their own expense, in cities as merchants and tradesmen in Our Residence St. Petersburg or in the neighboring cities of Livland, Estonia, Ingermanland, Carelia and Finland, as well as in the Residential city of Moscow, shall enjoy 5 years of tax-exemption. Moreover, each one who comes to Russia, not just for a short while but to establish permanent domicile, shall be granted free living quarters for half a year.

3. All foreigners who settle in Russia either to engage in agriculture and some trade, or to undertake to build factories and plants will be offered a helping hand and the necessary loans required for the construction of factories useful for the future, especially of such as have not yet been built in Russia.

4. For the building of dwellings, the purchase of livestock needed for the farmstead, the necessary equipment, materials, and tools for agriculture and industry, each settler will receive the necessary money from Our treasury in the form of an advance

loan without any interest. The capital sum has to be repaid only after ten years, in equal annual instalments in the following three years.

5. We leave to the discretion of the established colonies and village the internal constitution and jurisdiction, in such a way that the persons placed in authority by Us will not interfere with the internal affairs and institutions. In other respects the colonists will be liable to Our civil laws. However, in the event that the people would wish to have a special guardian or even an officer with a detachment of disciplined soldiers for the sake of security and defense, this wish would also be granted.

6. To every foreigner who wants to settle in Russia We grant complete duty-free import of his property, no matter what it is, provided, however, that such property is for personal use and need, and not intended for sale. However, any family that also brings in unneeded goods for sale will be granted free import on goods valued up to 300 rubles, provided that the family remains in Russia for at least 10 years. Failing which, it be required, upon its departure, to pay the duty both on the incoming and outgoing goods.

7. The foreigners who have settled in Russia shall not be drafted against their will into the military or the civil service during their entire stay here. Only after the lapse of the years of tax-exemption can they be

required to provide labor service for the country. Whoever wishes to enter military service will receive, besides his regular pay, a gratuity of 30 rubles at the time he enrolls in the regiment.

8. As soon as the foreigners have reported to the Guardianship Chancellery or to our border towns and declared their decision to travel to the interior of the Empire and establish domicile there, they will forthwith receive food rations and free transportation to their destination.

9. Those among the foreigners in Russia who establish factories, plants, or firms, and produce goods never before manufactured in Russia, will be permitted to sell and export freely for ten years, without paying export duty or excise tax.

10. Foreign capitalists who build factories, plants, and concerns in Russia at their own expense are permitted to purchase serfs and peasants needed for the operation of the factories.

11. We also permit all foreigners who have settled in colonies or villages to establish market days and annual market fairs as they see fit, without having to pay any dues or taxes to Our treasury.

VII. All the afore-mentioned privileges shall be enjoyed not only by those who have come into our country to settle there, but also their children and descendants, even though these are born in Russia, with the provision that their years of exemption will be reckoned from the day their forebears arrived in Russia.

VIII. After the lapse of the stipulated years of exemption, all the foreigners who have settled in Russia are required to pay the ordinary moderate contributions and, like our other subjects, provide labor- service for their country. Finally, in the event that any foreigner who has settled in Our Empire and has become subject to Our authority should desire to leave the country, We shall grant him the liberty to do so, provided, however, that he is obligated to remit to Our treasury a portion of the assets he has gained in this country; that is, those who have been here from one to five years will pay one-fifth, whole those who have been here for five or more years will pay one-tenth. Thereafter each one will be permitted to depart unhindered anywhere he pleases to go.

IX. If any foreigner desiring to settle in Russia wishes for certain reasons to secure other privileges or conditions besides those already stated, he can apply in writing or in person to our Guardianship Chancellery, which will report the petition to Us. After examining the circumstances, We shall not hesitate to resolve the matter in such a way that the petitioner's confidence in Our love of justice will not be disappointed.

Appendix II:

The Instructions of Catherine II to the Legislative Commission of 1767

1. The Christian Law teaches us to do mutual Good to one another, as much as possibly we can.

2. Laying this down as a fundamental Rule prescribed by that Religion, which has taken, or ought to take Root in the Hearts of the whole People; we cannot but suppose that every honest Man in the Community is, or will be, desirous of seeing his native Country at the very Summit of Happiness, Glory, Safety, and Tranquility.

3. And that every Individual Citizen in particular must wish to see himself protected by Laws, which should not distress him in his Circumstances, but, on the Contrary, should defend him from all Attempts of others that are repugnant to this fundamental Rule.

4. In order therefore to proceed to a speedy Execution of what We expect from such a general Wish, We, fixing the Foundation upon the above first-mentioned Rule, ought to begin with an Inquiry into the natural Situation of this Empire.

5. For those Laws have the greatest Conformity with Nature, whose particular Regulations are best adapted to the Situation and Circumstances of the People for whom they are instituted. This natural Situation is described in the three following Chapters.

Chapter I

6. Russia is a European State.

7. This is clearly demonstrated by the following Observations: The Alterations which Peter the Great undertook in Russia succeeded with the greater Ease, because the Manners, which prevailed at that Time, and had been introduced amongst us by a Mixture of different Nations, and the Conquest of foreign Territories, were quite unsuitable to the Climate. Peter the First, by introducing the Manners and Customs of Europe among the European People in his Dominions, found at that Time such Means as even he himself was not sanguine enough to expect.

Chapter II

8. The Possessions of the Russian Empire extend upon the terrestrial Globe to 32 Degrees of Latitude, and to 165 of Longitude.

9. The Sovereign is absolute; for there is no other authority but that which centers in his single Person that can act with a Vigour proportionate to the Extent of such a vast Dominion.

10. The Extent of the Dominion requires an absolute Power to be vested in that Person who rules over it. It is expedient so to be that the quick Dispatch of Affairs, sent from distant Parts, might make ample Amends for the Delay occasioned by the great Distance of the Places.

11. Every other Form of Government whatsoever would not only have been prejudicial to Russia, but would even have proved its entire Ruin.

13. What is the true End of Monarchy? Not to deprive People of their natural Liberty; but to correct their Actions, in order to attain the supreme Good.

14. The Form of Government, therefore, which best attains this End, and at the same Time sets less Bounds than others to natural Liberty, is that which coincides with the Views and Purposes of rational Creatures, and answers the End, upon which we ought to fix a steadfast Eye in the Regulations of civil Polity.

15. The Intention and the End of Monarchy is the Glory of the Citizens, of the State, and of the Sovereign.

16. But, from this Glory, a Sense of Liberty arises in a People governed by a Monarch; which may produce in these States as much Energy in transacting the most important Affairs, and may contribute as much to the Happiness of the Subjects, as even Liberty itself.

Chapter III

17. Of the Safety of the Institutions of Monarchy.

18. The intermediate Powers, subordinate to, and depending upon the supreme Power, form the essential Part of monarchical Government.

19. I have said, that the intermediate Powers, subordinate and depending, proceed from the supreme Power, as in the very Nature of the Thing the Sovereign is the Source of all imperial and civil Power.

20. The Laws, which form the Foundation of the State, send out certain Courts of judicature, through which, as through smaller Streams, the Power of the Government is poured out, and diffused.

21. The Laws allow these Courts of judicature to remonstrate, that such or such an Injunction is unconstitutional, and prejudicial, obscure, and impossible to be carried into Execution; and direct, beforehand, to which Injunction one ought to pay Obedience, and in what Manner one ought to conform to it. These Laws undoubtedly constitute the firm and immoveable Basis of every State.

[Author's note: Chapters VII and VIII, on punishments and the appointment of justices, has been trimmed for space.]

Chapter XIX

439. Of the Composition of the Laws

447. Every subject, according to the order and Place to which he belongs, is to be inserted separately in the Code of Laws -for instance, under judicial, military, commercial, civil, or the police, city or country affairs, etc.

448. Each law ought to be written in so clear a style as to be perfectly intelligible to everyone, and, at the same time, with great conciseness. For this reason explanations or interpretations are undoubtedly to be added (as occasion shall require) to enable judges to perceive more readily the force as well as use of the law...

449. But the utmost care and caution is to be observed in adding these explanations and interpretations, because they may sometimes rather darken than clear up the case; of which there are many instances [in the existing laws].

450. When exceptions, limitations, and modifications are not absolutely necessary in a law, in that case it is better not to insert them; for such particular details generally produce still more details.

451. If the Legislator desires to give his reason for making any particular law, that reason ought to be good and worthy of the law....

452. Laws ought not to be filled with subtle distinctions, to demonstrate the brilliance of the Legislator; they are made for people of moderate capacities as well as for those of genius. They are not a logical art, but the simple and plain reasoning of a father who takes care of his children and family.

453. Real candor and sincerity ought to be displayed in every part of the laws; and as they are made for the punishment of crimes, they ought consequently to include in themselves the greatest virtue and benevolence.

454. The style of the laws ought to be simple and concise: a plain direct expression will always be better understood than a studied one.

455. When the style of laws is tumid and inflated, they are looked upon only as a work of vanity and ostentation....

511. A Monarchy is destroyed when a Sovereign imagines that he displays his power more by changing the order of things than by adhering to it, and when he is more fond of his own imaginations than of his will, from which the laws proceed and have proceeded.

512. It is true there are cases where Power ought and can exert its full influence without any danger to the State. But there are cases also where it ought to act according to the limits prescribed by itself.

513. The supreme art of governing a State consists in the precise knowledge of that degree of power, whether great or small, which ought to be exerted according to the different exigencies of affairs. For in a Monarchy the prosperity of the State depends, in part, on a mild and condescending government.

514. In the best constructed machines, Art employs the least moment, force, and fewest wheels possible. This rule holds equally good in the administration of government; the most simple expedients are often the very best, and the most intricate the very worst.

515. There is a certain facility in this method of governing: It is better for the Sovereign to encourage, and for the Laws to threaten....

519. It is certain that a high opinion of the glory and power of the Sovereign would increase the strength of his administration; but a good opinion of his love of justice will increase it at least as much.

520. All this will never please those flatterers who are daily instilling this pernicious maxim into all the sovereigns on Earth, that Their people are created for them only. But We think, and esteem it Our glory to declare, that "We are created for Our people." And for this reason, We are obliged to speak of things just as they ought to be. For God forbid that after this legislation is finished any nation on Earth should be more just and, consequently, should flourish more than Russia. Otherwise, the intention of Our laws would be totally frustrated; an unhappiness which I do not wish to survive.

521. All the examples and customs of different nations which are introduced in this work [the Instruction] ought to produce no other effect than to cooperate in the choice of those means which may render the people of Russia, humanly speaking, the most happy in themselves of any people upon the Earth.

522. Nothing more remains now for the Commission to do but to compare every part of the laws with the rules of this Instruction.

Appendix III:

Declaration Upon the First Partition of Poland (1772)

The States bordering upon Poland have so often been involved in the disorders which have arisen during interregnums in that kingdom, that the experience of the past would in any case have led the neighboring powers to occupy themselves seriously with the affairs of that State the moment that the throne became vacant by the death of King Augustus III. This consideration and the obvious necessity of preventing the fatal effects of dissensions which threatened to arise with this last vacancy of the throne, led the Court of St. Petersburg to endeavor to bring about a union in favor of a candidate who should be at once the most worthy of the throne, and the most suitable to the interests of his fellow-citizens and of the neighboring States. It endeavored at the same time to rectify certain abuses in the constitution of the Polish State.

The Court of Berlin seconded the measures of its ally, while the Court of Vienna, although anxious to co6perate in assuring the success of these praiseworthy measures, believed it best on account of the embarrassments which might arise from increasing the number of those interfering directly in the domestic affairs of Poland, to remain neutral in this matter as well as in the war which sprang from it between Russia and the Ottoman Port.

As a result of these measures, the powers had the satisfaction of seeing the free and legal election of

King Stanislaus, who is now reigning, as well as other useful results. Everything seemed to promise a firm peace for both Poland and her neighbors, but unhappily the spirit of discord took possession of a portion of the nation, and destroyed in an instant all these hopes. Citizens armed themselves against one another, factions usurped the legitimate authority, which they abused in utter contempt of law, good order, and public security. justice, the police, commerce, yes, agriculture itself, all were destroyed.

The natural connection between Poland and her neighbors led them to feel most keenly the sad effects of these disorders. They have been forced for a long time to take the most costly measures in order to assure the tranquility of their own frontiers, and they are exposed, owing to uncertainty of what may result from the destruction of this kingdom, to the danger of the decline of the friendship and harmony which now exists among them. Nothing is consequently more urgent than a prompt remedy for these ills, which are producing the most vexatious effects in the neighboring states, and which, if no measures of prevention are taken, will probably entail modifications of the political system of this part of Europe.

Reasons of such weight forbid his Majesty the King of Prussia, her Majesty the Empress, Queen of Hungary and Bohemia, and her Imperial Majesty of all the Russias longer to defer taking a decisive stand in so critical a situation. These powers have agreed accordingly to attempt to reach without loss of time a common understanding, in order to restore peace and good order in Poland, and establish the ancient constitution of this State and the liberties of the nation upon a sound basis.

But while they have been able to prevent for the moment the ruin and the arbitrary destruction of this kingdom, owing to the friendship and good intelligence which now exists among them, they have had no assurance that they would meet with equal success in the future. They all had considerable claims upon various possessions of the republic. They could not allow these to be abandoned to the course of events; they consequently determined to enforce their ancient rights and legitimate claims on the possessions of the republic, - claims which each is ready to justify in due time and in the proper place.

Consequently his Majesty the King of Prussia, her Majesty the Empress, Queen of Hungary and Bohemia, and her Imperial Majesty of all the Russias, having mutually set forth their rights and claims, and having come to an agreement, will each take an equivalent of the district to which they lay claim, and will put themselves in effective possession of those portions of Poland which are calculated to serve hereafter as the most natural and secure boundary between them. Each of the three powers reserves the privilege of issuing a statement in due time, by which their Majesties will renounce hereafter all rights, claims, and pretensions for damages or interest which they may have upon the possessions and subjects of the Republic.

His Majesty the King of Prussia, her Majesty the Empress, Queen of Hungary and Bohemia, and her Majesty the Empress of all the Russias believe it their duty to announce their intentions to the whole Polish nation, requesting them to banish, or at least suppress, the spirit of disorder, so that the nation, coming together legally, can concert in the diet with the three courts in regard to the means for re6stablishing order and tranquility, as well as to confirm by formal acts the exchange of titles and claims of each of the powers to those regions of which they have just taken possession.

Further Reading

Catherine the Great: Portrait of a Woman, by Robert K. Massie

The Memoirs of Catherine the Great, translated by Mark Cruise and Hilde Hoogenboom

Instructions of Catherine the Great

> http://academic.shu.edu/russianhistory/index.php/Catherine_the_Great%27s_Instructions_to_the_Legislative_Commission%2C_1767

Correspondence of Catherine the Great and Voltaire

> http://aofe.pbworks.com/f/Catherine+the+Great+-+Voltaire+Letters.pdf

Letter from Baron de Breteuil

http://sourcebooks.fordham.edu/halsall/mod/18catherine.asp

Manifesto of Catherine II on Immigration

http://www.norkarussia.info/catherines-manifesto-1763.html

Catherine II Instructions

http://academic.shu.edu/russianhistory/index.php/Catherine_the_Great%27s_Instructions_to_the_Legislative_Commission%2C_1767

Partition of Poland

http://www.shsu.edu/~his_ncp/PartPol1.html

Decree on the Serfs, 1767

http://sourcebooks.fordham.edu/mod/18catherine.asp

Made in the USA
Middletown, DE
28 June 2020

11353260R00094